LUNCH IS ON THE TABLE!

Other Books by Robert Ackart

Breakfast Is Ready! 1996

Dinner Is Served! 1996

Please Help Yourself! 1996

The Pinstripe Gourmet 1986

Spirited Cooking 1984

The Frugal Fish 1983

A Celebration of Soups 1982

Soufflés, Mousses, Jellies, and Creams 1980

The Cheese Cookbook 1978

A Celebration of Vegetables 1977

The One-Dish Cookbook 1975

Fruits in Cooking 1973

Cooking in a Casserole 1973

The Hundred Menu Chicken Cookbook 1972

LUNCH IS ON THE TABLE!

40 Complete Menus with Step-by-Step Recipes for Midday Enjoyment

ROBERT ACKART

FG
FINLEY GREENE PUBLICATIONS, INC.

This book is available at a special
discount when ordered in bulk quantities.
For information, contact Special Sales Department,
Finley/Greene Publications, Inc.,
23 Alabama Avenue, Island Park, NY 11558.

Library of Congress Cataloging-in-Publication Data

Ackart, Robert C.
Lunch Is on the Table!

Includes index.
1. Cookery. I. Title.
ISBN 1-887678-03-4 (paperback)
ISBN 1-887678-02-6 (hardcover)

Printed in U.S.A.

Printing number

10 9 8 7 6 5 4 3 2 1

Contents

Introduction

THESE LUNCH MENUS ARE COMPRISED OF DISHES WHICH, EVEN HAD YOU TIME, YOU might not undertake during your busy weekly round. The recipes are not complicated—every effort has been made to assure that they are not—but the menus do present, it is hoped, somewhat unusual fare. Enjoy their preparation and consummation either at midday or, if you prefer, as light evening meals.

Because of my childhood upbringing, I feel that times spent as a group, either as family or with friends, are important—particularly in this day of helter-skelter activity on the parts of us all. A companionable time at midday is good cement for binding family relations and for learning to know friends better.

From the point of view of your children's exposure to dishes not offered at school or available to the local drive-in, perhaps these lunches constitute a painless education for future enjoyment of many different kinds of foods. (As children, my twin sister and I were served small portions of everything Mother had set on the table, and we were required to eat them. Often we returned for a second helping; more important, we grew up without food prejudices.) I mention food-adventuring because a degree of culinary sophistication will make meals easier to plan and happier for your family to share.

Terms, Hints, and How-to's for Use in This Book

PLEASE READ THIS SECTION OF THE BOOK; I FEEL IT WILL MAKE YOUR TIME IN THE kitchen pleasanter and easier.

First, a few general instructions.

The length of time needed to prepare the dishes and the length of time needed to cook them are suggested at the start of individual recipes. The preparation time is approximate, will vary with the expertise of the cook, and includes the peeling, chopping, and other readying of ingredients. It is assumed that, whenever possible, two or three steps in the preparation will be simultaneously undertaken. The cooking time usually refers to the period needed to finish the assembled dish, often following the suggestion *"At this point you may stop and continue later."* This direction is often included when recipes may be made either in one session or, if preferred, in two; it is omitted when the recipe is more effectively prepared in a single period. If you use the direction, remove the dish from the refrigerator so that it is at room temperature before you continue with the recipe at hand. If a recipe is oven-cooked, the temperature setting is indicated at the outset, so that your oven will be ready when you need it. Ingredients are listed in order of their use, and for cooks who (like myself) arrange their spice shelf alphabetically, herbs and seasonings are listed in that way.

If a recipe appears in more than one menu, it is given in its entirety the first time, and then cross-referenced by page number in later menus. (In each menu the page cross-reference occurs only once, in the initial menu listing. Any later references to the recipe title within that menu are capitalized to remind you that you can find that recipe either by looking again at the page reference at the beginning of the menu or by consulting the alphabetical index in the back of the book.)

Recipes for sauces that are used frequently in these menus are also found in this section, since to repeat them every time they are cited would lead to too much repitition and take up space better utilized for original recipes.

Most Important: Read all recipes for each menu to be sure you have on-hand all the necessary ingredients.

Now for the terms that follow. The subjects are entered alphabetically and cross-referenced where necessary. The entries give definitions for terms used in recipes, such as *roux* and *bouquet garni*; expressions and terms that we have adopted from foreign cuisines. Many entries deal with "how-to"—how to defat dishes or prepare seasoned flour, for example.

Almonds, toasted: On an ungreased baking sheet, evenly spread blanched whole or slivered almonds. In a 350° F. oven, bake them, turning them occasionally with a spatula, for about 12 minutes, or until they are a rich golden brown. Allow them to cool and "dry" before proceeding with the recipe at hand. Any unused toasted almonds will keep for several months, closely covered, in the refrigerator.

Bouquet garni: A selection of herbs and/or spices loosely tied together in cheesecloth and simmered with other ingredients to give added flavor. The cheesecloth bag facilitates discarding the seasonings once used and prevents the herbs from coloring or flecking the liquid. *Bouquets garnis* can (and should) be largely a product of your imagination, but to start you off, here are two that I find useful. One: 2 bay leaves, 2 whole cloves, 1 clove garlic, peeled and split, 8 sprigs of parsley, 6 peppercorns, ½ teaspoon thyme. Two: 2 bay leaves, 3 celery tops with leaves, ½ teaspoon marjoram, 4 sprigs of parsley, ½ teaspoon sage, 1 teaspoon summer savory. One can always add rosemary leaves, and a piece of lemon or orange zest lends a delightful nuance.

Butter: Sweet (unsalted) every time! Why? Personal prejudice—and because it does not add its taste to what is being cooked, only good richness. In these recipes, if you prefer to use margarine, by all means do so—just avail yourself of the best possible quality of unsalted oleomargarine in order to avoid any margarine taste. If you are happier with margarine, when it is recommended to use half butter and half cooking oil for browning meats, use all margarine. But do remember that the amount of fat is the same in oleo as in butter, though oleo, of course, not being animal fat, has no cholesterol.

Cheese, grated: I urge you—no, I beg you—for the greater pleasure you will derive from the recipes in which you use grated cheese, to grate it yourself rather than buying the commercially packaged kind, which does not taste or feel or look like freshly prepared cheese. If you have a food processor, buy a chunk of cheese, cut it into ¾-inch cubes, and, using the steel blade, drop them singly into the container of the processor. Granted, the cheese is not grated; it is ground, but it works beautifully in recipes calling for it. Do not try to grind such hard cheeses as Parmesan or Romano in the container of a blender; you will burn out the motor. But, lacking a processor, you have a strong arm and the desire to keep physically fit; grating cheese the old-fashioned way will tone muscle and contribute greatly to the appeal of the recipe at hand.

Chicken breasts: Breasts cook more rapidly than other portions of the bird's anatomy: baked in a sauce at 350° F., breasts are ready in 40 minutes (no more, else they will become dry and stringy); breasts baked, well coated with oil or melted butter, require only 10 to 15 minutes, depending upon their size, in a 425° F. oven; sautéing requires only 3 or 4 minutes per side.

Court bouillon: A savory liquid, slightly acid, made for cooking fish, court bouillon gives added flavor and retains the color of the fish. Herewith a suggested court bouillon for you to use in preparing fish recipes calling for it: 2 medium carrots, scraped and sliced thin; 6 sprigs of parsley; 8 scallions, trimmed and chopped, with some of the green part; 2 bay leaves, crumbled; 8 peppercorns; ½ teaspoon thyme; ¾ teaspoon salt; 4 cups water; and 2 cups dry white wine. In a saucepan, combine the ingredients, bring the liquid to the boil, reduce the heat, and simmer the mixture, covered, for 30 minutes. Strain it for use as a poaching liquid; afterward, reserve it as the basis for a soup or sauce. It can be kept for 10 days in the refrigerator and I've frozen it for as long as six months.

Curry: Curry, or curry powder, may be a combination of as few as twelve herbs and spices or as many as fifty. The name probably derives from an Indian word, *kari*, meaning sauce. It also refers to the dishes that Indians have been eating for 5,000 years. The ingredients were originally chosen for their medicinal and antiseptic properties, as well as for their flavor. Turmeric is a basic for color and flavor; hot chilies are used, as are ginger, garlic, cloves, cumin, coriander, and so forth. Various curry powders are available, but I urge you to seek out sweet Madras curry powder; it has a mellow flavor, rather than the sharp edginess discernible in more commercial brands. You will be pleased at the difference it makes in your completed dish.

Defatting: To defat a casserole-prepared recipe, make the dish 24 hours in advance of serving it. Refrigerate it overnight and the following day remove the fat, which will have solidified. This step is particularly helpful with dishes which cannot be made without creating a layer of fat on the top of the casserole. To defat canned chicken broth, refrigerate the can overnight; the following day the solidified fat will be strained out as you pour the chilled broth through a fine sieve.

Doubles; refrigerates; freezes; and [sometimes] halves: You will find any of the first three of these indications that may apply to the recipe at hand immediately following the preparation and/or cooking time. An indication that the menu can be halved is found after the recipes in the menu are listed. Many recipes (and menus) will double without presenting problems in final taste or consistency. You should allow yourself more preparation and cooking time (but not a great deal more) and larger utensils; and you might be prepared to stretch the sauce—should one be involved—by adding a bit more liquid to it with, perhaps, a little *beurre manié* to give it proper thickening.

Many completed recipes can be refrigerated overnight and served the next day; some refrigerate for family use as leftovers; others are refrigerated overnight to facilitate the removal of any solidified fat (I am all for *lean* meat dishes). Allow the dish to come fully to room temperature before heating it to serve or completing the recipe at hand.

Many recipes are purposely designed as the make-ahead-freeze-and-thaw-and-heat-to-serve variety. What a help they are to the busy homemaker! Again, many leftovers may be frozen for family use at a later date; you may not want to eat *coq au vin* two days running. In using frozen recipes, allow the dish to come fully to room temperature before heating it to serving temperature in a moderate (about 325°-350° F.) regular oven or in the microwave. Some foods (crêpes, breads, pastries, soups) can be frozen for almost six months, thawed to room temperature, and used. Soups may separate in thawing; whirl them in a blender (for chilled soups) or heat them gently, and they will reconstitute themselves.

Halving menus and recipes for two persons is perhaps a little trickier than doubling them. Somehow, sauces seem to shrink in quantity, or their consistency is not what you expect, or the principal ingredient becomes suddenly preponderant. If you are prepared to make the necessary culinary adjustments, I have suggested for halving to two servings only those menus originally intended for four persons, and which, I feel, will require a minimum effort, if any, on your part.

Dress (to season cooked vegetables): First, always season vegetables after cooking them; they will taste fresher for doing so. Second, never overcook vegetables; they should be cooked *à point* (*al dente,* if you will), so that there is a *bit* of resistance when you chew them and not the feeling that you are mouthing mush. To dress cooked frozen vegetables, such as chopped broccoli or spinach, Brussels sprouts, lima beans, green beans or peas, and so forth, melt in a largish saucepan about 1 tablespoon butter per 10-ounce package of frozen vegetable (or for an equal amount of fresh); add to the butter a little salt (or, preferably, a little fresh lemon juice), a fresh grinding of pepper, and, if desired, a splash of Pernod (which enhances the taste of many vegetables). Then to the contents of the saucepan, add the cooked, drained vegetable and, with a rubber spatula, gently fold together the seasonings and vegetable to blend the flavors well. Transfer the prepared vegetable to an ovenproof serving dish and heat it for serving, covered, in the oven or microwave. This is an easy method for making your vegetables flavorful, one that will leave you unharried at the time of serving.

To dress salads for serving, add to the prepared greens the suggested sauce or one of your choice (generally, about 1/3 cup); using two wooden spoons or salad servers, gently toss the mixture until the greens are evenly coated. Do not overuse the sauce; an oily salad is unpleasant, and more sauce can always be added if necessary.

Egg whites: If a recipe calls for only the yolks of eggs, do not despair that the whites will be wasted. Freeze them for later use in soufflés or mousses. Frozen, egg white keeps as long as six months and can be thawed and refrozen without spoiling.

Eggs, Poached: It is virtually impossible to poach more than 4 eggs at a time. If everyone wants 2 eggs, urge animated conversation while you prepare the second lot; or use two skillets.

In a large skillet, combine 4 cups water with 2 tablespoons cider vinegar and 1 teaspoon salt, if desired. This acidulated water will tend to hold the egg together; otherwise it may spread out in the pan. Bring the liquid to the simmer. Gently break each of 4 eggs into the simmering water and allow them to cook for about 4 minutes, or until the white is firm but not hard and the yolk is covered with a thin layer of the cooked white. With a slotted spoon, arrange each egg on a piece of toast.

Egg "poachers" are available. Actually, they are not poachers at all, but rather steamers—little cups that hold 1 egg each and that rest on a rack over simmering water. Eggs prepared this way are less risky than those prepared as suggested above (not so much chance of broken yolks, for example) and the taste is just as good, although the acidulated water adds the slightest piquancy of flavor, which I enjoy.

Fish: My personal preference is for lean-fleshed fish fillets (cod, flounder, haddock, halibut, scrod, sole, snapper, turbot) that come from the fishmonger clean and ready to use. Their flavor is delicate and full. If more convenient, use frozen fish. I allow it to thaw in the refrigerator before proceeding with the recipe at hand.

The Canadian Department of Fisheries has made a useful discovery, one that eliminates all chance from cooking fish, which should be done as quickly as possible in order to preserve both texture and flavor: Lay the fish on a flat surface and measure it at its deepest point. For each inch of depth, allow 10 minutes of cooking in simmering water for poaching, in a hot (400°–450° F.) oven for baking, or in a preheated broiler. If you roll fish fillets, measure the depth *after* you have rolled them. For unthawed frozen fish, double the time per inch of depth.

Freezes: see *Doubles; refrigerates; freezes; and [sometimes] halves.*

Garlic: Like scallions, chives, and onions, garlic is a member of the lily family (I know, you don't believe me, but it's true). It was extolled by Hippocrates and by Alcuin, Charlemagne's mentor and herbalist. Peeling garlic cloves is made easier either by giving the clove a gentle whack with the broad side of a heavy knife or by pouring boiling water over it. Today, available in the produce department of your supermarket is bottled chopped garlic in oil. While I continue to put garlic through a press and occasionally to chop it, this product is a welcome time-saver.

Halves: see *Doubles; refrigerates; freezes; and [sometimes] halves.*

Julienne: A French culinary term meaning fine-cut vegetables, meats, or fruit rinds. Julienne of carrots, for example, consists of pieces about the size of a wooden matchstick; julienne of ham is cut about half as thick as a lead pencil; and julienne of fruit zest (the outer, oily part of the skin of a lemon or orange) is very fine indeed, about 3/32 of an inch (but you do not have to measure).

Lemon-Parsley Sauce (for meats, fish, poultry, and vegetables)

Yield: about 2 cups
Preparation and cooking: about 25 minutes
Refrigerates

4 tablespoons butter
4 tablespoons flour
1 cup canned chicken broth
1 cup light cream
Salt, if desired
Fresh-ground white pepper

1. In a saucepan, heat the butter and in it, over gentle heat, cook the flour for a few minutes. Gradually add the liquid ingredients, stirring constantly until the mixture is thickened and smooth. Season it to taste with salt and pepper.

Grated rind and strained juice of 1 medium lemon (about 2 tablespoons)
¼ to ⅓ cup fine-chopped parsley

2. Into the contents of the saucepan, stir the lemon rind and juice and parsley. Over very gentle heat, simmer the sauce for a few minutes.

Light cream: Although light cream is called for in these recipes, you may use as well half-and-half, which seems more prevalent in supermarkets than its more venerable cousin.

Mornay Sauce (for poultry, fish, and vegetables)

Yield: about 2½ cups
Preparation and cooking: about 15 minutes

Doubles; refrigerates; freezes

4 tablespoons butter
4 tablespoons flour
Grating of nutmeg
½ teaspoon salt
Fresh-ground white pepper

1. In a saucepan, heat the butter and in it, over gentle heat, cook the flour for a few minutes. Stir in the seasonings.

2 cups milk
¼ cup grated Gruyère cheese
¼ cup grated Parmesan cheese
1 teaspoon Worcestershire sauce, if desired

2. To the contents of the saucepan, gradually add the milk, stirring constantly until the mixture is thickened and smooth. Away from the heat, add the cheese, stirring until it is melted. Stir in the Worcestershire sauce.

Mushrooms: The name covers a wide variety of edible fungi. In about 400 B.C. the Greek Hippocrates referred to the popularity of mushrooms, indicating that they were even exported. For centuries, the cooking of France, Germany, Russia, and Italy has made use of mushrooms; they have been an ingredient of oriental cuisines since very early time.

Until fairly recently, the only mushroom readily available was the white variety farmed commercially. This member of the large family of edible fungi still remains the cook's standby. But at the market one also sometimes finds *cèpes* and morels, considerably more flavorful that the *champignons de Paris*, as our common mushroom is known to French cooks, and also at times *porcini* and *portobelli*, delicious Italian fungi. By all means avail yourself of these rarer examples *if* you find them in a reliable store. Because poisening from eating the *wrong* mushroom can be exceedingly dangerous, leave experimenting to mycologists, knowledgeable students of fungi.

To prepare them as a cooked garnish, wipe the mushrooms with a damp paper towel; trim and slice or quarter them (as a garnish, they should be in reasonably small segments). In a saucepan, combine 2 tablespoons each butter, strained fresh lemon juice, and water. Heat the mixture until the butter is melted; add the mushrooms, tossing them lightly with a rubber spatula to coat them well. Over low heat, cook the mushrooms, covered, for 5 minutes. Drain them, if desired, or add them together with their liquid to the dish at hand.

Mushrooms may be wiped, trimmed, and sliced a day ahead. To prevent them from darkening fold into them strained lemon juice.

Mustard Sauce (for meats, poultry, and fish)

Yield: about 1½ cups

Preparation and cooking: about 15 minutes

1½ tablespoons butter
1½ tablespoons flour
¾ cup canned chicken broth, defatted
1 envelope chicken bouillon powder
⅓ cup heavy cream
1 tablespoon Dijon mustard

In a saucepan, heat the butter and in it, over gentle heat, cook the flour for a few minutes. Gradually add the chicken broth and bouillon, stirring constantly until the mixture is thickened and smooth. Stir in the cream and allow the mixture to come to a simmer. Add the mustard, stirring to blend the sauce well.

FOR VARIATION:
Horseradish Sauce: In place of the mustard, stir into the thickened mixture 4 tablespoons prepared horseradish, pressed dry in a sieve; add a few drops Worcestershire sauce.

Onions, white, to peel: Cut a thin bit off the root end of each onion. Drop the onions into briskly boiling water for 1 minute only; do not cover them. Drain and refresh them in cold water. Redrain them. The skins will slip off easily when you pinch the top end of the onion. Please note that this method of dealing with white onions will not work for the common garden variety of yellow onion (a staple ingredient in many recipes), which must be peeled by hand and then chopped—a tearful business, unless you buy frozen chopped onion. If you do use the frozen onion, allow extra cooking time to evaporate the water content.

Paprika: A red powder condiment prepared from one variety of capsicum, or sweet pepper, originally from South America, but which found its way to Hungary in the latter sixteenth century. Paprika may vary in mildness or sharpness and in its degree of sweetness. Hungarian paprika is less sharp and sweeter than that ordinarily found on supermarket shelves; it is worth your searching out. All dishes in this book calling for paprika are better-tasting for being made with it.

Parsley, to chop: With a scissors, cut off the leaves into a measuring cup (or pinch them off). Hold the cup so that you can put the cutting blades of the scissors into it and still snip comfortably. Cut through the parsley leaves until they are as fine as you want them. My phrase, "fine-chopped parsley," does not mean pulverized; the herb should still be recognizable as such. Parsley may also be chopped in the container of a food processor, but have a watchful eye or you will end up with a sort of green paste; also, the measuring-cup-scissors method requires less washing up.

Poach: To poach chicken breasts or fish, in simmering water or *court bouillon* (above) barely to cover, cook the chicken breasts or fish, uncovered, for about 5 to 8 minutes. Do not overcook. Chicken breasts are done when they are resilient to the prick of a fork; fish fillets, when they flake easily but are still firm. Remove the poached meat at once from the heat and allow it to cool in the poaching liquid.

Refrigerates: see *Doubles; refrigerates; freezes; and [sometimes] halves.*

Reheating: see "*Doubles, refrigerates,*" above

Rice: Rice or bulgur gives a meal a bit of weight without making it heavy. Both are quickly and easily prepared; they are very nutritious; they are tasty; and they are a challenge to your culinary creativity. For these reasons, they are often used in this book as a meal-time staple.

Rice, the source of about 80 percent of the calories for nearly one-half the world's population, is one of our oldest cultivated crops, probably brought from southern India to Europe by the armies of Alexander the Great. It was grown in China, however, as far back as 5000 B.C. and in Egypt from 400 B.C. onward. Arabs brought it to Spain, whence it came to the Western world with the Spanish explorers. It found its way to North America, or more specifically to North Carolina, in 1685, where it rapidly became a valuable crop. Carolina-grown rice evolved as the standard of quality for rice produced around the world. In point of fact, the Carolina regions discontinued rice-growing around 1865, but to this day the term "Carolina rice" continues as a synonym for the highest quality of long-grain rice.

The Chinese and Hindus believed rice to be a symbol of fertility and from this concept comes our custom of throwing rice at a bride and groom, indicating a wish that they may have children.

The edible rice kernel is found at the center of a hull surrounded by several layers of bran. In the case of brown rice, nearly all the bran is retained and for this reason it has more flavor and is more nutritionally valuable than highly refined, branless milled or polished rice, the varieties most commonly found at your supermarket. (Wild rice, incidentally, is not rice at all, but a grain related to the wheat family; it grows uncultivated in the swamp waters of the northern Lake States, particularly Minnesota and Wisconsin. By law, only Indians of the area are permitted to gather it. Its delicious nut-like flavor and interesting texture make it a culinary delicacy—together with its forbiddingly high cost—the result of its being harvested by hand.)

Bulgur or, sometimes, bulghur, is parched cracked wheat from which some of the bran has been removed.

Rice and bulgur are cooked in identical ways. (Wild rice is prepared quite differently and, when serving it, you will do well to follow the cooking instructions on the package.) I prefer raw natural rice to the "converted" or precooked varieties; cooking raw natural rice, from start to finish, requires at most only 20 minutes, and the results are both tasty and consistent.

A rule of thumb for cooking raw natural rice, brown rice, and bulgur is: for each cup of grain (which when cooked will yield 4 servings), heat in a saucepan 1 tablespoon butter or oil; add the rice or bulgur, stirring to coat each grain (this step helps prevent the grains from sticking together); add 2 cups water or other liquid and ¾ teaspoon salt; over high heat, bring the liquid to the boil, stir the grain once with a fork, reduce the heat, and simmer the rice or bulgur, covered, for about 15 minutes, or until it is tender and the liquid is absorbed. (Brown rice will require about 50 minutes cooking time.)

Raw natural rice, brown rice, and bulgur may also be oven-cooked in a casserole: in place of the saucepan, use a flameproof casserole with a tight-fitting lid. Proceed with the basic instructions as written, above. In a saucepan, bring the cooking liquid to the boil; add it to the prepared grain in the casserole; stir it once with a fork and then bake the grain, covered, at 350° F. for 18 to 25 minutes (for raw natural rice and bulgur) or 45 to 50 minutes (for brown rice).

Nothing could be simpler. And the variations you can play on these themes are virtually endless. For example, you may want to cook a small onion or clove of garlic, peeled and chopped fine, in the butter before stirring in the rice or bulgur. You may stir into the grain before adding the cooking liquid any one of the following:

¾ teaspoon ground allspice
¾ teaspoon basil
1 bay leaf, crumbled
¾ teaspoon chervil
1 to 1½ teaspoons curry powder
¾ teaspoon dill weed
¾ teaspoon marjoram

Grated rind of 1 small orange
½ teaspoon rosemary
½ teaspoon saffron
½ teaspoon sage
½ teaspoon thyme
¾ teaspoon turmeric

And you may vary the cooking liquid. Flavor the water with a chicken or beef bouillon cube or a packet of bouillon powder (in these cases, omit the salt). In place of water, use chicken, beef, or vegetable broth. Combine water and strained fresh orange juice to equal 2 cups. Use half broth and half dry white wine. Always remember that you will need 2 cups of liquid for 1 cup of grain.

Last, for added flavor and visual appeal, at the time of serving, you may stir into the cooked grain:

⅓ cup toasted slivered almonds
⅓ cup currants
¼ cup chopped dates
2 tablespoons fine-chopped fresh mint
1 cup sliced sautéed mushrooms
½ cup chopped pitted ripe olives
⅓ cup grated Parmesan or Romano cheese
¼ to ½ cup fine-chopped parsley
¼ cup chopped pimiento
½ cup thoroughly drained pineapple tidbits
¼ cup pine nuts (pignoli)
3 tablespoons poppy seeds
⅓ cup seedless raisins
¼ to ½ cup scallions, trimmed and chopped fine, with some of the crisp green part
1 large ripe tomato, peeled, seeded, chopped, and drained
¼ cup fine-sliced water chestnuts
⅓ cup fine-chopped watercress leaves

To incorporate these flavorful additions, use two forks and toss the rice lightly with the garnish of your choice.

Roux: Equal quantities of fat (usually butter) and flour, the butter heated and the flour added to it; the two are then cooked together over gentle heat to eliminate any graininess and mealy taste. *Roux* is used as a thickening agent for sauces and soups. If desired, the flour may be cooked in the butter until it darkens, thus lending color to the sauce.

Rubber spatula: A rubber spatula is the most helpful of all the weapons I wield in the kitchen; it mixes, it blends, it gets all of the sauce out of the pan, it folds a soufflé without deflating it. Rubber spatulas and measuring cups are the chief constituents of my *batterie de cuisine*.

Salad greens and garnishes: It is difficult, if not impossible, to specify the quantity of various lettuces and garnishes (cherry tomatoes, scallions, etc.) that you will need for salads. First, the size of the completed salad will depend upon appetites. Second, except for iceberg lettuce (which provides a pleasant crisp-sweet accent to salads), head lettuces such as Bibb and Boston vary widely in the density of their leaves. Sometimes, for example, one head of Boston lettuce will serve four, while at other times two heads will be needed. Fortunately, salad greens and garnishes keep well in the "crisper" section of the refrigerator. Store unused leaves rinsed, drained as dry as possible, and packed loosely in a plastic bag. The quantity of salad greens suggested in the recipes is an approximation of what you will need for a medium serving per person; a gently squeezed head of lettuce or one weighed in hand should be your final guide.

Salt, salting: Unless a recipe truly requires it, I have indicated "Salt, if desired," while substituting for NaCl a sprinkling or a more specific amount of lemon juice, or light-grated rind. Lemon, like salt, brings out flavors *and*, unlike salt, adds its own element of healthfulness.

In my kitchen, foods are usually prepared without salt and are seasoned after the recipe is completed—whenever possible without reverting to salt. I urge you to try this approach for your pleasure at table; once free of the salt habit, you will find foods taking on flavors and bouquets that you had not realized were theirs. Your pleasure in eating will become greater—and your food healthier. (See also Dress [to season cooked vegetables], above.)

Scald: Scalding milk or cream prevents their souring when in contact with other ingredients. To scald milk or cream easily, it is not necessary to bring it to a boil—and watch in alarm as it bubbles, lava-like, onto the stove! Heat the milk or cream until they seem to have a glazed appearance and shimmer (not simmer). *Voilà!* Whenever possible, milk or cream can be scalded in the utensil you will continue using for the recipe at hand, just to save on washing up.

Seasoned flour: In a waxed paper or plastic bag, shake together 2/3 cup flour, 1 teaspoon salt, and ½ teaspoon white pepper (white, so that the resultant sauce will not be speckled). To the contents of the bag, add, a few pieces at a time, the meat to be floured. Holding the bag tightly closed, shake it vigorously to dredge the meat; remove the meat, shaking back into the bag any excess flour. Add a bit of the seasoned flour to the recipe when making the sauce.

Note: if you add to the recipe the juice of 1 small lemon (a practice that I recommend for salt-conscious cooks), you may wish to omit the salt altogether; to the flour add instead a grating of nutmeg, a little paprika, or a pinch of powdered thyme.

Shallots: Scallions, sometimes called green onions, and shallots are milder than their cousins. Shallots grow like onions—but not as one main bulb, rather as an aggregate, breaking apart easily like garlic cloves. Native to Western Asia, their name is a corruption of "Ascalon," a Philistine city, and they probably were taken to Western Europe by returning Crusaders. So much for history! For our purposes, the mild, slightly sweet flavor of shallots yields a more delicate dish than robust yellow onions; for this reason, I sometimes suggest them. When they are not available, scallions are recommended as a satisfactory substitute.

Soufflés, chilled: A boon to the busy homemaker who wants to offer a festive dessert but who simply cannot cope with creating one at 5:45 in the afternoon. Answer: make a chilled soufflé a day ahead. Recipes for various of these airy pleasures are scattered throughout the book; the Index also lists them so that you may pick and choose which you would most like to serve.

Sour cream (a substitute for): In the container of a food processor or blender, combine 2 cups small-curd cream-style cottage cheese, 2 tablespoons strained fresh lemon juice, and 2 tablespoons non-fat milk. Whirl the mixture until it is smooth (it will have the slightest graininess— rather pleasant). Refrigerate it, tightly covered, for up to 2 weeks.

In the dairy section of your supermarket, you will find various "light" (calorie-reduced) sour cream preparations. These can be substituted for the regular product.

Vegetables, cooking of: A list of "don'ts." Don't overcook vegetables. Don't salt the water in which they are cooked; season them when done. Don't drown them; cook them in as small an amount of liquid as possible. Don't tarry over the cooking of them; prepare them as rapidly as possible. Rewards: more flavor, greater crispness, and a greater measure of their nutrients preserved.

Without shame, I encourage you to use frozen vegetables. Those called for in these menus and recipes are admirable stand-ins for fresh ones, which are not always available and which would require your time in preparing before cooking them. Frozen vegetables, pan-ready and cooked according to the suggestions above, will relieve you of end-of-day kitchen labor and will speed your meal to the table.

Vinaigrette Sauce (for salads and vegetables)

Yield: about 1¼ cups
Preparation: about 10 minutes

Doubles; refrigerates

½ teaspoon salt
¾ teaspoon sugar
½ teaspoon white pepper
1 teaspoon Dijon mustard
2 tablespoons very hot water
4 tablespoons vinegar of your choice

1. In a container with a tight-fitting lid, combine and shake together these ingredients until the salt and sugar are dissolved.

¾ cup olive or vegetable oil

2. To the contents of the container, add the oil and continue shaking the mixture until it is thoroughly blended.

Lemon Vinaigrette Sauce (for salads and vegetables)

Yield: about 1½ cups
Preparation: about 10 minutes

Doubles; refrigerates

6 tablespoons strained fresh lemon juice
½ teaspoon Dijon mustard
1 teaspoon sugar
½ teaspoon salt
½ teaspoon white pepper

1. In a container with a tight-fitting lid, combine and shake these ingredients until the salt and sugar are dissolved.

¾ cup olive or vegetable oil

2. To the contents of the jar, add the oil and shake the mixture until it is thoroughly blended.

FOR VARIATION:
Orange Vinaigrette Sauce (for fruit salads and spicy greens): In place of the lemon juice, use strained fresh orange juice and add the lightly grated rind of 1 orange.

Zest: The outermost rind of citrus fruits, which contains the flavorful oils. To remove the zest, use a vegetable peeler; avoid the white part of the skin, which is bitter. The zest of limes, lemons, and oranges gives a concentrated flavor of the fruit and can be used in various ways to enhance many recipes.

Orange zest prepared as garnish: (a festive and tasty topping for many desserts) Cut the zest of 1 medium orange into julienne (see above). In a small saucepan, cover the julienne strips with cold water, bring the liquid to the boil, reduce the heat, and simmer the strips, uncovered, for 5 minutes. Drain and reserve them for use as needed. To prepare orange zest for desserts, cut it in julienne "twigs," as suggested above. In a saucepan, combine 1 cup water and 1 cup sugar. Bring the mixture to the boil and cook it, uncovered, for 5 minutes. Add the orange julienne, reduce the heat, and simmer it, uncovered, for 5 minutes. With a slotted spoon, remove the zest to a plate and allow it to cool and dry. Sprinkle the sweetened zest over the dessert in question.

Complete Menus for Lunches

YOU MAY WELL ASK, "IF AN ENTIRE MENU IS SUGGESTED, WHY NOT A WINE TO accompany it?" My answer is, "Simply because many people (I among them) have certain preferred wines which are appropriate and satisfying." If you wish to experiment, you will find that serious wine-shop proprietors are an excellent source of guidance in your selection. Barring their assistance, your own palate will be your best advisor, more reliable than the airy hyperbole often found in syndicated wine columns describing the pleasures afforded by a given grape or vineyard. If a recipe calls for wine, I recommend that you offer the same one to accompany the completed dish. I urge, too, that you eschew so-called "cooking wine"; your dish should be *enhanced* by the wine you use in it.

You will find in these recipes an unashamed use of canned, frozen, and other convenience foods. Because the underlying idea of the book is ease of preparation and, in so far as possible, a modicum of time spent in the kitchen, it would be pointless to suggest, for example, that you prepare your own chicken stock. To you who might wish to make everything "from scratch" (and I often do), I say: Bravo! But for those of us to whom relaxed kitchen time is an elusive luxury, I offer easier and less time-consuming ways of preparation without loss of quality.

A reminder: These menus are only suggestions. You may, and should if you wish, mix and mingle recipes from other menus.

Sautéed Chicken Breasts for 4

Sautéed Chicken Breasts
Orange Rice
Green Bean Salad with Red Onion in Vinaigrette Sauce (page xxv)
Raspberry Sherbet

(Menu Halves)

A day ahead:

prepare the vinaigrette sauce and refrigerate it

cook the green beans

prepare step 1 of the rice recipe

In the morning:

complete step 2 of the green bean salad

Sautéed Chicken Breasts

Yield: 4 servings
Preparation: about 5 minutes
Cooking: about 6 minutes
Doubles

2 full skinless, boneless chicken breasts, trimmed of all fat and halved lengthwise
Seasoned flour

1. With absorbent paper, pat the chicken dry and then dredge it lightly in the seasoned flour; shake off any excess flour.

3 tablespoons butter
1 tablespoon vegetable oil

2. In a skillet, heat the butter and oil and, over medium-high heat, cook the chicken until it is golden (about 3 minutes); turn the pieces and repeat; do not overcook them.

Fine-chopped parsley
Lemon wedges

3. Transfer the breasts to a heated serving plate and garnish them with parsley and lemon wedges.

Orange Rice

Yield: 4 servings
Preparation: about 10 minutes
Cooking: 25 minutes
Doubles

2 tablespoons butter
2 shallots, peeled and chopped fine, *or* 2 scallions, trimmed and chopped fine, the white part only
1 cup raw natural rice
Grated rind of 1 medium orange
2 tablespoons strained fresh lemon juice
Fresh-ground white pepper

1. In a saucepan, heat the butter, and in it, over medium heat, cook the shallots until they are translucent. Add the rice, stirring to coat each grain. Stir in the orange rind, lemon juice, and a grinding of pepper.

At this point you may stop and continue later. (Refrigerate the saucepan with the rice, covered.)

2 cups strained fresh orange juice

2. Into the contents of the saucepan, stir the orange juice. Bring the liquid to the boil, stir once again, reduce the heat, and simmer the rice, covered, for 15 minutes, or until it is tender and the liquid is absorbed.

Green Bean Salad with Red Onion in Vinaigrette Sauce

When shopping, look for the youngest beans possible (thinnest, shortest); if you cannot find them, cut large ones into 3-inch segments.

Yield: 4 servings
Preparation: about 55 minutes
Chilling time: at least 3 hours
Doubles; refrigerates

Salt, if desired
Water
1 pound green beans, the stem ends trimmed, rinsed

1. In a soup kettle, bring to the boil several quarts of lightly salted water. Add the beans and cook them, uncovered, for about 8 minutes *after* the water has returned to a gentle boil; test them as they cook (they should be tender-crisp). Drain and refresh them in cold water; drain again and then dry them on absorbent paper.

If desired, you may arrange the beans, all lying parallel to each other, in a neat grouping on a serving platter. An attractive way to serve the salad.

At this point you may stop and continue later. (Cover the beans with plastic wrap and refrigerate them.)

1 medium red onion, peeled, cut into thin rings, and separated
Fine-chopped parsley
½ to ⅔ cup Vinaigrette Sauce

2. Over the beans, arrange the onion rings. Sprinkle the salad with parsley. Refrigerate the salad until you wish to serve it. Over all, slowly drizzle the Vinaigrette Sauce.

If you are preparing this recipe for 6 persons, use 1½ pounds green beans.

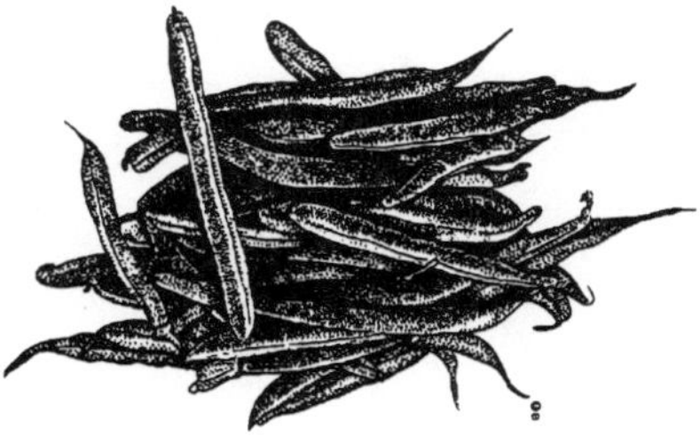

Chilled Salmon Mousse for 6

Chilled Salmon Mousse
Mixed Vegetable Salad
Gougère or Muffins
Blueberries in Cassis or Strawberries with Orange-Flavored Liqueur
Cookies of Your Choice

Most of the recipes in this menu can be adjusted to serve 8.

The *gougère* does not double in the making. If you are offering this menu to 8 persons, I suggest you serve muffins (page 35) in place of the *gougère.*

A day ahead:

make the salmon mousse

prepare the mixed vegetable salad

prepare, fold, and refrigerate the blueberries with the cassis *or*

prepare and refrigerate the strawberries, but do not toss them with the liqueur

In the morning:

measure out all the ingredients for the *gougère*

About two hours ahead:

fold the strawberries with the liqueur

Chilled Salmon Mousse

If desired, the recipe may be made with 2 (7-ounce) cans of water-pack tuna, drained, in place of the salmon.

Yield: 6 to 8 servings
Preparation: about 30 minutes
Chilling time: at least 6 hours
Refrigerates

1. Lightly oil and chill a 6-cup ring or other mold.

1½ envelopes unflavored gelatin, softened for 5 minutes in ¼ cup strained fresh lemon juice
Grated rind of 1 medium lemon
¾ cup boiling water

2. To the gelatin, add the lemon rind and boiling water, stirring until the gelatin is dissolved; reserve it.

2 cups cream-style cottage cheese
1 small onion, peeled and grated
2 (7-ounce) cans salmon, drained and broken into chunks
½ teaspoon paprika
A few drops of hot-pepper sauce
Reserved gelatin

3. In the container of a food processor or blender, combine these six ingredients and whirl them until the mixture is smooth. Transfer it to a mixing bowl.

⅓ cup fine-chopped celery
¼ cup fine-chopped gherkins
⅔ cup mayonnaise

4. To the contents of the mixing bowl, add the celery, gherkins, and mayonnaise. Blend the mixture well and chill it until it just begins to set.

1 cup heavy cream, whipped

5. Fold in the whipped cream. Using a rubber spatula, transfer the mixture to the chilled mold. Chill the mousse for at least 6 hours, or until it is thoroughly set.

Mixed Vegetable Salad

Allow 3 (10-ounce) packages frozen mixed vegetables for 6 persons. Cook the vegetables as directed on the package; do not overcook them. Refresh them in cold water and drain them well. In a mixing bowl, using a rubber spatula, blend them with just sufficient mayonnaise (about ½ cup) to bind the mixture; season the salad with a little strained fresh lemon juice and fresh-ground white pepper. Chill the salad for 3 hours and offer it as a side dish on greens of your choice.

FOR VARIATION:
Mixed Vegetable Salad, Vinaigrette: Dress the salad with Lemon Vinaigrette Sauce, page xxv, to taste, which complements the vegetables nicely.

If you are preparing the recipe for 4 persons, 2 (10-ounce) packages frozen mixed vegetables will be adequate. If you are making the salad for 8 persons, use 4 packages vegetables.

Unmold the mousse onto a chilled serving platter and garnish it with the mixed vegetable salad.

Gougère

This tasty Burgundian cheese puff is a delightful accompaniment to light meals.

Yield: 6 servings
Preparation: about 15 minutes

Cooking: 25 minutes in a 375° F. oven; 10 minutes at 350° F.

1 cup water
6 tablespoons butter
1 teaspoon Dijon mustard
¼ teaspoon salt, if desired
1 cup flour

1. In a saucepan, combine the water and butter. When the mixture just begins to boil, add the mustard and salt and then, all at once, the flour. Over low heat, stir the mixture vigorously until the pastry draws away from the sides of the pan and forms a ball.

4 eggs
1 cup (4 ounces by weight) shredded Gruyère *or* Emmenthaler cheese

2. Away from the heat, to the flour mixture, add the eggs separately, beating each addition until it is entirely incorporated in the pastry. Stir in the cheese.

3. Around the edge of a well-buttered 10-inch pie plate, arrange the dough in mounds. Bake the *gougère* at 375° F. for 25 minutes; reduce the heat to 350° F. and continue baking it for 10 minutes longer. Cut it into 6 wedge-shaped pieces and serve them at once.

Blueberries in Cassis or **Strawberries with Orange-flavored Liqueur**

Two (1-pint) boxes of blueberries *or* a 1-quart box of strawberries will yield an adequate dessert serving for 6 persons; for 8, you may want to purchase another pint.

Stem, rinse, and drain the blueberries. In a mixing bowl, combine them with about 1/3 cup *crème de cassis* (black currant liqueur); use more, if necessary, for 8 servings. With a rubber spatula, fold them with the liqueur to coat them well. Transfer them to a serving bowl and refrigerate them, covered with plastic wrap, for at least 3 hours. Their flavor improves with being prepared a day ahead.

Hull, rinse, and drain the strawberries. If they are very large, halve or quarter them. About 2 hours before serving them, fold them, as suggested above, with about 1/3 cup orange-flavored liqueur; again, use more, if necessary, for 8 servings. Chill them. (Strawberries will discolor and go mushy if combined with a liqueur too many hours before being served.)

Offer the berries with cookies of your choice.

Spinach Soufflé for 4

Spinach Soufflé
Sautéed Mushrooms
French Bread
Fresh Pineapple with Ginger and Amaretto

A day ahead:

trim the mushrooms, if necessary, and refrigerate them covered with plastic wrap

prepare the pineapple

prepare steps 1, 2, and 3 of the soufflé recipe

Spinach Soufflé

Yield: 4 servings
Preparation: about 25 minutes
Cooking: about 40 minutes (30 minutes in a 350° F. oven)

1. Thoroughly butter a 2-quart soufflé dish.

4 tablespoons butter
4 tablespoons flour
Grating of nutmeg
½ teaspoon salt, if desired
Fresh-ground pepper
1 cup milk

2. In a saucepan, heat the butter and in it, over gentle heat, cook the flour for a few minutes. Stir in the seasonings. Gradually add the milk, stirring constantly until the mixture is thickened and smooth. Remove it from the heat.

1 (10-ounce) package frozen chopped spinach, fully thawed to room temperature
1 teaspoon strained fresh lemon juice
4 egg yolks (refrigerate the whites)

3. In a sieve, press the spinach with a flat spoon to extract as much liquid as possible. Stir the spinach into the contents of the saucepan. Add the egg yolks and, with a spoon, beat the mixture until the yolks are thoroughly incorporated into the batter.

At this point you may stop and continue later. (Refrigerate the saucepan, covered, and the soufflé dish. If you are doing this a day ahead, be sure that the batter is fully at room temperature before continuing with the recipe.)

4 or 5 egg whites at room temperature, beaten until stiff but not dry

4. Beat the spinach mixture until it is smooth. Into the contents of the saucepan, beat one-fifth of the egg white; fold in the remainder. Using a rubber spatula, transfer the mixture to the prepared dish. Bake the soufflé at 350° for 30 minutes, or until it is well puffed and golden. Serve it at once.

For other flavor accents: omit the nutmeg and add to the thickened butter-flour-milk mixture 3 tablespoons grated Parmesan cheese; or 1 medium onion, peeled and grated; or 1½ to 2 teaspoons prepared horseradish.

Sautéed Mushrooms

Yield: 4 to 6 servings
Preparation: about 10 minutes
Cooking: about 7 minutes

3 tablespoons butter
1 pound button mushrooms, trimmed if necessary
Strained fresh lemon juice
Fresh-ground pepper
¼ cup fine-chopped parsley

In a skillet (or Chinese *wok*, which is ideal for this kind of cooking), heat the butter and in it, using two spoons or salad paddles, toss the mushrooms to coat them well. Over medium heat, cook them, covered, for about 5 minutes, or until they are just tender. Season them to taste with lemon juice and pepper. Transfer them to a heated serving dish and sprinkle them with parsley.

Fresh Pineapple with Ginger and Amaretto

For 4 servings use a pineapple that weighs about 2 pounds.

1. With a sharp knife, cut off the ends of the pineapple. Cut the pineapple in lengthwise halves, then in quarters, and finally in eighths. Cut the rind from each section; cut away and discard the core (you will be able to distinguish it from the flesh of the fruit by its texture and slightly different color); cut out any black eyes that may have remained from removing the rind. Last, cut the sections into bite-size pieces and reserve them.

2. In a mixing bowl, combine the pineapple segments with ¼ cup amaretto, ½ to ¾ teaspoon powdered ginger, and 3 tablespoons candied ginger, chopped fine. Using a rubber spatula, toss the fruit to coat it well with the liqueur and to blend it with the ginger. Transfer it to a serving dish and chill it for at least 3 hours.

Antipasto Lunch for 6 to 8

Antipasto Platter with Quick Tuna and Bean Salad
Italian Bread with Butter
Fresh Pineapple with Citrus Juice

An attractively arranged platter of antipasto accompanied by good Italian bread and sweet butter makes an appetizing meal in any season. The slightly tart pineapple gives a pleasant ending to this light lunch.

Because antipasto is so versatile it also stands one in good stead as part of a buffet for a larger group.

A day ahead:

make the tuna and bean salad; cover it with plastic wrap and refrigrate it

hard-cook the eggs (allow 1 per serving) but do not peel them; refrigerate them

prepare the pineapple

prepare the lettuce and refrigerate it in a plastic bag

Antipasto

Preparation: about 20 minutes Doubles; refrigerates

2 medium heads Boston lettuce, rinsed and spun dry
Boiled ham slices, rolled
Italian salami, sliced thin
Rolled anchovies, thoroughly drained
Hard-cooked eggs, peeled, halved lengthwise, and garnished with a little mayonnaise
Ripe pitted olives
Scallions, trimmed
Cherry tomatoes *or* tomato slices

On a serving platter, arrange a bed of lettuce. On it, arrange the ham rolls, salami, anchovies, eggs, olives, scallions, and tomatoes. Be sure to leave room on the platter for . . .

Quick Tuna and Bean Salad

Yield: 6 to 8 servings Doubles; refrigerates
Preparation: about 15 minutes

2 (19-ounce) cans white kidney beans, drained and rinsed in a colander
1 (7-ounce) can tuna fish in oil, drained and mashed with a fork
¼ cup fine-chopped parsley
4 tablespoons olive oil
Strained fresh lemon juice
Fresh ground white pepper
Salt, if desired

In a mixing bowl, combine the beans, tuna fish, parsley, and olive oil. Using two forks, gently toss the mixture to blend the ingredients well, seasoning them to taste with lemon juice and pepper and salt, if desired. The salad may be served slightly chilled or at room temperature. Add the salad to the antipasto platter.

If you wish, you may spruce up the salad, before you toss it, by the addition of one or more of the following:

2 celery stalks, trimmed and diced
1 small cucumber, peeled, quartered lengthwise, seeded, and diced
½ green pepper, seeded and chopped fine
1 medium red onion, peeled and chopped fine

Fresh Pineapple with Citrus Juice

Yield: 6 servings
Preparation: about 20 minutes
Chilling time: at least 3 hours
Refrigerates

1 large ripe pineapple (about 3 pounds)

1. Prepare the pineapple as directed on page 11.

Strained juice of 1 medium orange (about 5 tablespoons)
Strained juice of 1 small lemon (about 1½ tablespoons)
¼ to ⅓ cup sugar (depending upon the desired degree of sweetness)

2. In a small mixing bowl, combine the juices and sugar, stirring to dissolve the sugar. Arrange the pineapple segments in a serving bowl. Over them, pour the liquid, tossing to coat them well. Cover the dessert with plastic wrap and refrigerate it for at least 3 hours.

Crab Salad in Avocado Halves for 6

Crab Salad in Avocado Halves
Cream Biscuits
Melon of Your Choice

A day ahead:

make the sauce (step 1) for the crab salad

prepare the watercress and refrigerate it in a plastic bag

prepare step 1 of the biscuit recipe

Crab Salad in Avocado Halves

Yield: 6 servings
Preparation. about 30 minutes
Chilling time: at least 3 hours
Doubles; refrigerates (overnight)

1½ teaspoons heavy cream
½ cup mayonnaise
3 tablespoons ketchup
½ teaspoon celery salt
½ teaspoon curry powder, if desired
2 teaspoons grated onion
2 tablespoons fresh lemon juice
1 tablespoon dry sherry
Fresh-ground white pepper

1. In a mixing bowl, combine and blend thoroughly all of these ingredients.

At this point you may stop and continue later. (Cover and refrigerate the sauce overnight.)

1½ pounds chilled cooked fresh lump crabmeat, the tendons removed

2. Using a rubber spatula, fold the crabmeat into the sauce; take care not to break up the lumps. Chill the salad for at least 3 hours.

3 large ripe avocados, halved lengthwise and seeded
Fresh lemon juice
Watercress, rinsed and drained well, the woody stems removed
¼ cup fine-chopped parsley

3. With a pastry brush, paint the avocado halves liberally with lemon juice to prevent their discoloring. Fill each cavity with crab salad. On a chilled platter, arrange a bed of watercress; over it arrange the avocado halves, and in the middle of the platter, spoon any remaining salad. Overall, sprinkle the parsley.

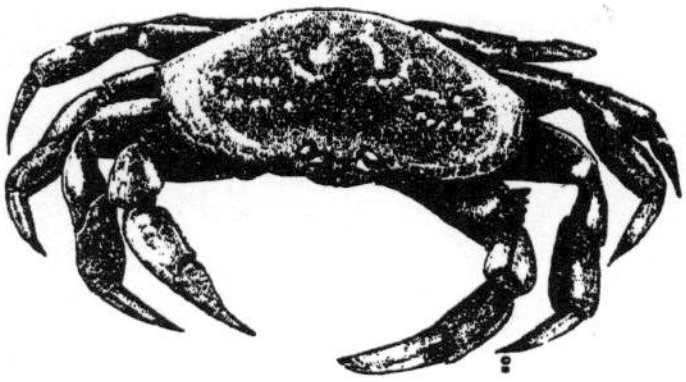

Cream Biscuits

Yield: 12 to 18 biscuits
Preparation: about 10 minutes

Cooking: 12 minutes in a 400° F. oven
Recipe halves

1½ cups flour
1 tablespoon baking powder
1 teaspoon salt

1. In a mixing bowl, sift together the dry ingredients.

At this point you may stop and continue later. (Cover and reserve the dry ingredients.)

1 cup heavy cream, at room temperature

2. Lightly butter a baking sheet. To the dry ingredients, add the cream; with a fork, stir the mixture only sufficiently to moisten the flour.

3. Drop the batter by the spoonful onto the baking sheet (the recipe yield will depend upon the size of spoon you use). Bake the biscuits at 400° F. for 12 minutes, or until they are well risen and golden.

FOR VARIATION:
Cream Biscuits with Lemon: Add, when stirring in the cream in step 2, the grated rind of 1 lemon.

Cream Biscuits with Orange: Add, when stirring in the cream in step 2, the grated rind of 1 orange.

Barley and Mushroom Casserole for 6

Garlic Soup
Barley and Mushroom Casserole
Chopped Spinach
Dried-Fruit Compote
Cookies of Your Choice

2 days ahead:
make the garlic soup

prepare steps 1, 2, and 3 of the barley casserole

A day ahead:
prepare step 1 of the spinach dish

make the dried-fruit compote

Garlic Soup

No, the garlic is not overpowering; actually, the soup is delicately flavored. Garlic numbers among the 400 herbs Hippocrates recommended for good health (most of which are still in use today, by the way); the ancient Romans thought it made warriors brave; and until the end of World War I it was considered an effective disinfectant for wounds. More important to our purposes, however, is the fact that things made with it taste good!

Yield: about 7 cups
Preparation and cooking: about 35 minutes

Doubles; refrigerates; freezes

1 medium bulb garlic (15 to 20 cloves)

1. Separate the garlic cloves and drop them into boiling water for about 5 seconds; drain them. Peel them; you will find that the skins slip off easily. Chop them coarse.

6 tablespoons butter
1 medium bunch parsley, rinsed, the heavy stems discarded

2. In a large saucepan, heat the butter and in it cook the parsley and garlic, stirring, until the parsley is limp.

4 tablespoons flour
3 (10½-ounce) cans defatted chicken broth

3. Into the garlic mixture, stir the flour and, over gentle heat, cook the mixture for a few minutes. Gradually add the chicken broth, stirring constantly until the mixture is thickened and smooth. Over gentle heat, simmer it, covered, for about 15 minutes; stir it often.

4. Allow the mixture to cool somewhat. In the container of a food processor or blender, whirl the mixture, about two cups at a time. until it is smooth. Transfer the purée to a saucepan.

2 cups milk, scalded
Strained fresh lemon juice
Fresh-ground white pepper

5. To the contents of the saucepan, add the scalded milk. Bring the soup to a gentle boil, stirring, before seasoning it to taste with lemon juice and pepper.

Barley and Mushroom Casserole

Yield: 6 servings
Preparation: about 25 minutes
Cooking: 1¼ hours (50 minutes in a 350° F. oven)
Doubles; refrigerates

6 tablespoons butter
1 pound mushrooms, trimmed and quartered
1 large onion, peeled and chopped fine

1. In a flameproof casserole, heat the butter and in it cook the mushrooms and onion until the onion is translucent.

1¼ cups medium pearl barley
½ teaspoon dill weed
½ teaspoon marjoram
½ teaspoon thyme
¾ teaspoon salt
½ teaspoon fresh-ground pepper

2. To the contents of the casserole, add the barley, stirring to coat each grain. Stir in the seasonings.

1½ cups strained fresh orange juice
1¼ cups tomato juice *or* tomato juice cocktail
Grated rind of 1 orange
Strained juice of 1 medium lemon (about 2 tablespoons)

3. In a saucepan, combine these four ingredients.

At this point you may stop and continue later. (Cover the barley casserole and the saucepan and refrigerate them.)

Fine-chopped parsley

4. Over high heat, bring the liquid ingredients to the boil. Pour them over the contents of the casserole. Bake the dish, covered, at 350° F. for 50 minutes, or until the barley is tender and the liquid is absorbed. Stir the dish occasionally as it cooks. Just before serving, garnish the casserole with parsley.

Chopped Spinach

Yield: 6 servings
Preparation: about 15 minutes
Cooking: 25 minutes in a 350° F. oven

3 or 4 (10-ounce) packages frozen chopped spinach, fully thawed to room temperature
Soft butter (about 4 tablespoons)
Strained fresh lemon juice (about 1½ tablespoons)
Fresh-ground pepper to taste
A little salt, if desired

1. In a sieve, press out as much liquid from the spinach as possible. In a mixing bowl, combine the spinach with the butter, lemon juice, and fresh-ground pepper. Using two forks, toss the mixture to blend it well. Arrange it in an ovenproof serving dish.

At this point you may stop and continue later. (Cover the dish and refrigerate it.)

2. Bake the spinach, covered, at 350° F. for 25 minutes.

If you are preparing the recipe for 4 persons, use 2 or 3 packages spinach; if you are serving 8, use 4 or 5 packages.

FOR VARIATION:
Chopped Spinach with Pernod: In step 1, add ¼ cup Pernod; complete the recipe as written.

Chopped Spinach with Scallions and Horseradish: In step 1, add 3 scallions, trimmed and chopped fine, and 1 tablespoon prepared horseradish. Complete the recipe as written.

Chopped Spinach with Mushrooms: In step 1, add ¼ pound mushrooms, and use two forks to toss them gently with the spinach.

Dried-Fruit Compote

Yield: 4 to 6 servings
Preparation and cooking: about 25 minutes
Chilling time: about 3 hours
Doubles; refrigerates

¾ cup sugar
1 cup water
Zest and juice of 1 medium lemon (about 2 tablespoons juice)
Zest and juice of 1 medium orange (about 5 tablespoons)
⅓ cup ruby port
4 allspice berries, bruised
1 (3-inch) piece cinnamon stick
4 whole cloves
A few grains of salt, if desired

1. In a saucepan, combine these ingredients. Over high heat, bring them to a rolling boil and cook the syrup, uncovered, for 5 minutes.

1 (11-ounce) package mixed tenderized dried fruit

2. To the syrup, add the dried fruit. Reduce the heat to medium and cook the fruit, covered, stirring occasionally, for about 20 minutes, or until it is tender but still retains its shape. With a slotted spoon, transfer it to a serving dish. Over the fruit, strain the syrup. Allow the compote to cool before chilling it.

FOR VARIATION:
Dried-Fruit Compote with Amaretto: Vary the compote by using ½ cup each of dry white wine and water, and add to the cooking fruit ¼ cup amaretto. Omit the ruby port. Serve the compote garnished with a dollop of sour cream.

Dried-Fruit Compote with Red Wine: Vary the compote by using 1⅓ cups dry red wine in place of the water and the ruby port; adjust the amount of sugar to taste.

Dried-Fruit Compote with White Wine: Vary the compote by using 1⅓ cups dry white wine in place of water and the ruby port; adjust the amount of sugar to taste.

Dried-Fruit Compote with Liqueur: Prepare the basic recipe and into the completed dish, while it is still hot, stir ¼ cup fruit-flavored liqueur of your choice.

Shrimp Salad for 4

Shrimp Salad
Gougère, page 8, or Cream Biscuits, page 15
Vanilla Ice Cream or Lemon Sherbet with Peaches
Cookies of Your Choice

If you offer the menu to 8 persons by doubling the recipes, I suggest you serve Cream Biscuits in place of the *gougère*.

A day ahead:

make steps 1 and 2 of the shrimp salad

hard-cook the eggs but do not peel them; refrigerate them

prepare the salad greens and refrigerate them in a plastic bag

complete step 1 of the biscuit recipe, if desired

In the morning:

measure all the ingredients for the *gougère*

prepare the peaches

Shrimp Salad

Yield: 4 servings
Preparation: about 45 minutes
Chilling time: at least 3 hours
Doubles; refrigerates (for 2 days)

1 pound medium raw shrimp
8 cups water
1 bay leaf
A few celery leaves
1 small onion, peeled and sliced
1 teaspoon salt, if desired

1. Shell and devein the shrimp. While you are doing so, bring to the boil and then let simmer, covered, the water to which are added the bay and celery leaves, the sliced onion, and the salt. When the shrimp are ready, return the water to a rolling boil. Add the shrimp and cook them, uncovered, for about 3 minutes, or until they turn pink; do not overcook them. Refresh them in cold water, drain them, and halve them lengthwise, if desired (not essential).

½ cup fine-chopped celery
½ cup thin-sliced water chestnuts
¼ cup fine-chopped scallions (with a little of the green part)
Mayonnaise (about ½ cup)
Strained fresh lemon juice
Fresh-ground white pepper

2. In a mixing bowl, combine the celery, water chestnuts, scallions, and shrimp. Toss them with sufficient mayonnaise to bind the mixture; season it to taste with lemon juice and pepper. Chill it for at least 3 hours.

Salad greens of your choice
12 cherry tomatoes, stemmed and halved
4 hard-cooked eggs, peeled and halved lengthwise

3. On a serving platter, arrange a bed of salad greens. Over them, spoon individual servings of shrimp salad. Garnish the platter with cherry tomatoes and the egg halves.

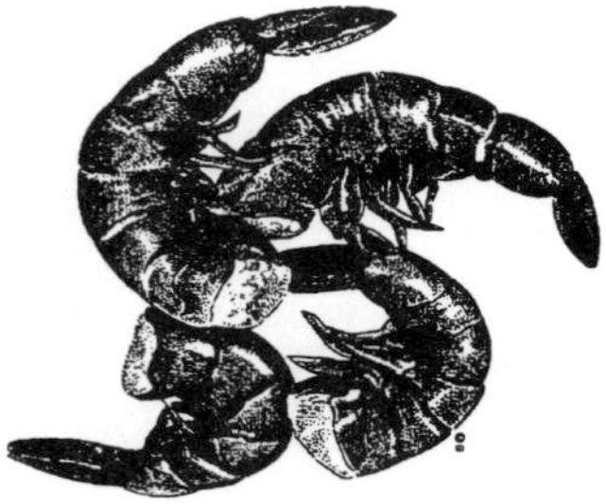

Vanilla Ice Cream or Lemon Sherbet with Peaches

If fresh peaches are in season, allow 1 medium ripe peach per serving. Peel and slice the peaches and, in a mixing bowl, toss them gently with a little (about 3 tablespoons) amaretto; chill the peaches before spooning them over individual servings of ice cream. (If you serve lemon sherbet, I think you will enjoy the peaches more if they are marinated in orange- flavored liqueur). If you happen to be serving this luncheon in the dead of winter, do not despair of the peaches: frozen sliced peaches, readily available, thawed and marinated as suggested, will substitute nicely.

Offer the dessert with cookies of your choice.

Meat Loaf for 6

Marinated Mushrooms
Meat Loaf with Lemon-Parsley Sauce (page xvii)
Bulgur Salad
Chilled Apple Mousse

The mushrooms may be served hot or offered chilled as a first course or as a side dish. The meat loaf may be served hot or chilled. Truly a do-ahead meal.

2 days ahead:

prepare the mushrooms

prepare the meat loaf for cooking and refrigerate it, covered with plastic wrap, or, if you wish to serve it chilled, complete the recipe

A day ahead:

make the salad

make the mousse

make the lemon-parsley sauce and refrigerate it

Marinated Mushrooms

Yield: 6 to 8 servings
Preparation: about 30 minutes
Marination time: 2 days
Doubles; refrigerates

¾ cup olive oil
⅓ cup strained fresh lemon juice
Zest of 1 medium lemon, chopped coarse
1 large clove garlic, peeled and split lengthwise
2 bay leaves
½ teaspoon oregano
½ teaspoon thyme
6 peppercorns
Salt, if desired
1½ pounds small mushrooms, stemmed (reserve the stems for use in another dish, such as Mushroom and Barley Soup)

1. In a saucepan, combine all the ingredients except the mushrooms. Bring the mixture to the boil, stirring. Arrange the mushrooms in a mixing bowl and over them pour the hot sauce. With a rubber spatula, fold the mushrooms with the sauce so that they are well coated. Cover the bowl and refrigerate the mushrooms for 2 days; stir the mushrooms occasionally so that they absorb the marinade evenly.

Salad greens of your choice, if desired

2. Drain the mushrooms and serve them on salad greens as a first course or chilled side dish; or heat them briefly in the marinade before draining them for use as a hot side dish.

Meat Loaf with Lemon-Parsley Sauce

Yield: 6 to 8 servings (any remaining meat loaf is good served chilled or sliced thin in sandwiches)

Preparation: about 20 minutes
Cooking: 1 hour in a 350° F. oven
Refrigerates

- **2 pounds lean ground beef**
- **1 cup bread crumbs**
- **1 egg, slightly beaten**
- **1 medium onion, peeled and chopped fine**
- **½ teaspoon basil**
- **½ teaspoon thyme**
- **¾ teaspoon salt, if desired**
- **Fresh-ground pepper**
- **Grated rind and strained juice of 1 medium lemon (about 2 tablespoons)**
- **¼ cup chicken broth**

1. In a mixing bowl, combine and blend thoroughly all of the ingredients. Pack the mixture into a lightly buttered 5 x 9-inch loaf pan.

At this point you may stop and continue later. (Cover the pan with plastic wrap and refrigerate it.)

2. Arrange the loaf pan on a baking sheet. Bake the meat loaf at 350° F. for 1 hour, or until it shrinks somewhat from the sides of the pan.

3. Run a knife around the edges of the loaf before turning it out onto a warmed serving platter. (Or, if you wish to serve it cold without the sauce, allow it to cool in the pan before refrigerating it, well covered with plastic wrap.)

Note: for the purposes of this menu, heat 1 recipe Lemon-Parsley Sauce during the final minutes of cooking the meat loaf, either over gentle heat or in the microwave oven; offer the sauce separately.

Bulgur Salad

Yield: 8 to 10 servings
Preparation: about 30 minutes
Chilling time: at least 3 hours
Doubles; refrigerates

2 cups coarse bulgur
6 cups lightly salted boiling water
Strained juice of 2 medium lemons (about 4 tablespoons)

1. In a mixing bowl, combine the bulgur, boiling water, and lemon juice. Allow the mixture to stand, covered, until it has reached room temperature. In a sieve, drain the bulgur thoroughly, pressing out any excess liquid with the back of a broad spoon.

12 scallions, trimmed and chopped fine, with as much of the green as is crisp, *or* 1 large red onion, peeled and chopped fine
1 cup fine-chopped parsley
3 medium ripe tomatoes, peeled, seeded, and chopped
⅓ cup olive oil, plus additional if necessary
Grated rind and strained juice of 1 medium lemon (about 2 tablespoons)

2. In a mixing bowl, combine the bulgur with the scallions, parsley, tomatoes, ⅓ cup olive oil, and lemon rind and juice. Using two forks, toss the mixture to blend it well. Add more olive oil if the salad seems dry. Refrigerate it for at least 3 hours.

⅓ cup fine-chopped fresh mint leaves (dill weed will substitute)

3. When serving the salad, garnish it with the chopped mint.

Chilled Apple Mousse

Yield: 6 to 8 servings
Preparation: about 30 minutes; about 1 hour setting time
Chilling time: at least 6 hours

1. Chill a 6-cup ring mold.

Grated rind and strained juice of 1 medium lemon (about 2 tablespoons)
4 large tart apples, peeled, cored, and cut into chunks

2. In the container of a food processor equipped with the steel blade, whirl the lemon rind, juice, and apple until the mixture is reduced to a smooth purée.

½ cup orange juice
1 envelope unflavored gelatin

3. Put the orange juice into the top of a double boiler. In the orange juice, soften the gelatin for 5 minutes; over simmering water, dissolve it in the top of the double boiler. Add the gelatin to the apple mixture.

⅔ cup sugar
¾ teaspoon powdered cinnamon
½ teaspoon nutmeg
1 teaspoon vanilla *or* 3 tablespoons amaretto

4. To the apple mixture, add the sugar, and seasonings. Whirl the ingredients until they are thoroughly blended and the sugar is dissolved. Transfer the mixture to a large bowl and chill it until it just begins to set.

1 cup heavy cream, whipped

5. With a rotary beater, whip the apple mixture briefly to assure its smoothness. Fold in the whipped cream. Rinse the chilled mold with cold water. Using a rubber spatula, transfer the mixture to the chilled mold. Chill the mousse for 6 hours, or until it is thoroughly set.

Chef's Salad Buffet for 8 to 10

Chef's Salad
Toasted English Muffins with Butter
Charlotte Russe

A day ahead:

prepare the salad greens and refrigerate them in plastic bags

prepare the tomatoes, eggs, chicken, and ham for the salad; refrigerate them in separate plastic bags

make the garlic vinaigrette sauce and refrigerate it

make the Charlotte russe

In the morning:

prepare the avocado

Chef's Salad

Combine the ingredients only when ready to serve the salad.

Yield: 8 to 10 servings — Preparation: about 50 minutes

3 large ripe tomatoes, peeled, seeded, and chopped
4 hard-cooked eggs, sliced
1 full skinless, boneless chicken breast, trimmed of all fat, poached and diced
1 (8-ounce) package boiled ham, cut into 2-inch julienne strips
1 large ripe avocado, peeled, seeded, cut into large dice, and tossed with fresh lemon juice (to prevent its discoloring)
1 medium head Boston lettuce
1 medium head red lettuce
1 medium head romaine lettuce
1 large bunch watercress, the woody stems removed
½ cup crumbled blue cheese
1 cup Vinaigrette Sauce (page xxv) mixed with 2 cloves garlic, peeled and put through a press

When you are ready to serve the salad, in a large salad bowl, combine all of the ingredients and gently toss them together until they are blended and well coated with the dressing. Serve the salad as soon as the English muffins are ready.

Charlotte Russe

Yield: 8 to 10 servings
Preparation: about 35 minutes; about 1 hour setting time
Chilling time: at least 6 hours

Ladyfingers (about 20)
¼ cup rum, Madeira, or Marsala

1. Line a 9-inch springform pan with split ladyfingers standing on end. Sprinkle them with the liquor of your choice.

2 envelopes unflavored gelatin
1 cup sugar

2. In the top of a double boiler, blend the gelatin and sugar.

3 cups milk
6 egg yolks

3. To the contents of the double boiler, add the milk and egg yolks; using a rotary beater, blend the mixture thoroughly. Over simmering water, cook the custard, stirring constantly, until it coats a metal spoon. Remove it from the heat and transfer it to a large mixing bowl.

2 tablespoons strained fresh lemon juice
1 tablespoon vanilla

4. Stir in the lemon juice and vanilla. Allow the mixture to cool before chilling it until it just begins to set.

2 cups heavy cream, whipped

5. Fold in the whipped cream. Pour the mixture into the springform pan, taking care that the ladyfingers remain upright. Chill the Charlotte russe for at least 6 hours, or until it is thoroughly set. Unmold the dessert onto a chilled serving plate and offer it in wedges (as you would cut a cake).

Scallop and Shrimp Risotto for 6

Scallop and Shrimp Risotto
Mixed Salad with Red Peppers with Vinaigrette Sauce (page xxv)
Sherbet of Your Choice
Cookies of Your Choice

A day ahead:

prepare step 1 of the risotto recipe

shell and devein the shrimp; if necessary, halve or quarter the scallops; refrigerate them, well covered

refrigerate the canned chicken broth

prepare the salad ingredients and refrigerate them in separate plastic bags

prepare the vinaigrette sauce and refrigerate it

Scallop and Shrimp Risotto

Yield: 6 servings
Preparation: about 30 minutes
Cooking: about 30 minutes

4 tablespoons butter
2 tablespoons olive oil
1 medium celery stalk, trimmed and chopped fine
1 small clove garlic, peeled and chopped fine
2 shallots, peeled and chopped fine, *or* 2 scallions, trimmed and chopped fine, with a little of the crisp green part
1½ cups raw natural rice

1. In a large saucepan, heat the butter and oil and, over medium heat, cook the celery, garlic, and shallots until the shallots are barely limp. Add the rice, stirring to coat each grain. Reserve the rice.

At this point you may stop and continue later. (Refrigerate the saucepan, covered.The ingredients for the risotto should be fully at room temperature before continuing with the recipe.)

1 (8-ounce) bottle clam juice
1 cup dry white wine
1 pound scallops (if you use sea scallops, halve or quarter them, according to their size)
1 pound medium shrimp, shelled and deveined
½ teaspoon crumbled saffron

2. In a saucepan, combine the clam juice and wine. Bring the liquid to the boil and add the scallops and shrimp; reduce the heat and simmer them, uncovered, for about 4 minutes, or until the shrimp are slightly pink; do not overcook them. Through a colander placed in a mixing bowl, strain out the seafood and reserve it; cover it to keep it moist. To the reserved liquid, add the saffron.

Defatted canned chicken broth, if needed
1 tablespoon Cognac
2 tablespoons strained fresh lemon juice
Salt, if desired
Fresh-ground white pepper

3. To the liquid, add chicken broth, if necessary, to equal 3 cups. Stir in the Cognac and the lemon juice. Season the broth with salt, if necessary, and to taste with pepper.

Reserved rice mixture

4. To the rice mixture, add the liquid, bring it rapidly to the boil; stir the rice once with a fork. Reduce the heat to low and simmer the rice, covered, for 15 minutes, or until it is tender and the liquid is absorbed.

Reserved seafood
¼ cup fine-chopped parsley
Grated Parmesan cheese

5. To the rice, add the seafood together with any accumulated liquid and the parsley. Using two forks, toss the mixture lightly to blend the ingredients. Transfer the risotto to a warmed serving dish and offer the Parmesan cheese separately.

Mixed Salad with Red Peppers, Vinaigrette

Combine to your taste 2 medium heads Boston or other leaf lettuce, endive (if available), thin-sliced mushrooms, and sweet red pepper, cut in julienne strips. Dress the salad with about 1/3 cup Vinaigrette Sauce.

Linguine My Way for 4

Linguine My Way
Mixed Salad with Endives
Fresh Fruit of Your Choice

(Menu Halves)

A day ahead:

prepare the salad ingredients and refrigerate them in separate plastic bags

prepare the vinaigrette sauce and refrigerate it

Linguine My Way

Yield: 4 servings
Preparation: about 10 minutes
Cooking: about 9 minutes
Doubles

4 eggs, beaten
4 tablespoons soft butter
3 or 4 cloves garlic, peeled and put through a press
½ cup grated Parmesan cheese
½ cup fine-chopped parsley
Fresh-ground pepper

1. In a large bowl suitable for tossing the pasta when it is cooked, combine these ingredients (I tend to be rather liberal with the pepper!)

At this point you may stop and continue later. (Refrigerate the sauce, covered; it must be fully at room temperature before adding the pasta to it.)

1 pound spinach linguine
Salt
Boiling water

2. In several quarts of lightly salted boiling water, cook the pasta according to the directions on the package until it is *al dente*; do not overcook it. Drain and add it to the sauce. Using two forks, toss the linguine with the sauce until it is well covered. Serve it directly onto heated plates; offer additional cheese separately, together with a pepper mill.

Mixed Salad with Endives

To 1 large head of Boston lettuce, rinsed and drained, add 1 medium endive, separated, 1 small red onion, peeled, sliced, and separated into rings, and cherry tomatoes, halved. Dress the salad with Vinaigrette Sauce, page xxv, about ⅓ cup.

Shrimp or Chicken Salad with Apples and Peas for 6

Mushroom and Barley Soup
Shrimp or Chicken Salad with Apples and Peas
Cream Biscuits, page 15
Dried-Fruit Compote, page 19

2 days ahead:

make the soup; refrigerate it, covered

A day ahead:

refrigerate the canned chicken broth

prepare all the ingredients for the salad (except the frozen peas) and refrigerate them separately

prepare step 1 of the biscuit recipe

make the compote

An hour ahead:

thaw the frozen peas; alternately, you may run warm water over them just before using

Mushroom and Barley Soup

Yield: 6 to 8 servings
Preparation and cooking: about 45 minutes

Doubles; refrigerates

3 tablespoons butter
1 medium carrot, scraped and sliced thin
1 medium rib celery, trimmed and diced
1 clove garlic, peeled and chopped fine
1 medium onion, peeled and chopped fine

1. In a large saucepan, heat the butter and in it, over medium heat, cook the vegetables until the onion is translucent.

1 pound mushrooms, trimmed and sliced thin

2. Add the mushrooms and continue to cook the mixture, stirring, until the mushrooms are coated with butter.

4 (10½-ounce) cans chicken broth, defatted
⅓ cup medium pearl barley
Strained fresh lemon juice
Fresh-ground pepper
Salt, if desired

3. To the contents of the saucepan, add the broth and barley. Bring the liquid to the boil, reduce the heat, and simmer the soup for 35 minutes, or until the barley is tender. Season the soup to taste with lemon juice, pepper, and, if necessary, a sprinkling of salt.

Shrimp or Chicken Salad with Apples and Peas

If desired, frozen cooked shrimp, fully thawed, may be substituted for the fresh.

Yield: 6 to 8 servings
Preparation: about 30 minutes
Chilling time: at least 3 hours
Doubles; refrigerates

1 pound fresh shrimp, shelled, deveined, and cooked (see page 21), *or* 1 full skinless, boneless chicken breast, trimmed of all fat, poached, and diced
3 large tart apples, peeled, cored, diced, and tossed with the strained juice of 1 lemon (about 2 tablespoons)
2 (10-ounce) packages frozen small peas, fully thawed to room temperature
1½ cups diced celery
½ medium green pepper, seeded and diced
6 scallions, trimmed and chopped fine, with a little of the green part
Mayonnaise (about ½ cup)
Salad greens of your choice

In a mixing bowl, combine all of the salad ingredients except the mayonnaise and the greens. Add sufficient mayonnaise just to bind the mixture. With a rubber spatula, fold the ingredients together to blend them well. Chill the salad for 3 hours before serving it on the greens.

Baked Shad Roe for 4

Baked Shad Roe
Watercress Salad with Mushrooms, Vinaigrette Sauce (page xxv)
Muffins
Poached Pears with Raspberry Sauce

(Menu Halves)

A day ahead:

prepare the watercress and refrigerate it in a plastic bag

make the vinaigrette sauce and refrigerate it

make the poached pears with raspberry sauce

prepare the mushrooms and refrigerate them in a plastic bag

In the morning:

prepare the shad roe for cooking and refrigerate it

thaw the raspberries

Baked Shad Roe

Yield: 4 servings
Preparation: about 15 minutes

Cooking: 15 minutes in a 400° F. oven

Soft butter
4 large shad roe (2 pairs)
8 tablespoons dry white wine
3 scallions, trimmed and chopped fine, with a little of the crisp green part
Paprika
Fresh-ground pepper
Fine-chopped parsley
Salt, if desired
Lemon wedges

With the butter, spread four squares of aluminum foil large enough to accommodate and seal each individual roe. In the center of each square, arrange a roe. Over each, pour 2 tablespoons wine; to each, add a sprinkling of scallions and of paprika and pepper. Garnish each roe with parsley. Draw the edges of the foil up and fold them to seal the roe lengthwise; seal the ends in the same way. Bake the roe at 400° F. for 15 minutes. Offer the roe opened but still in its foil nest, accompanied by a lemon wedge.

Watercress and Mushroom Salad

For 6 servings, use 2 large bunches watercress, rinsed, dried on absorbent paper, and the woody stems discarded. Use ½ pound mushrooms, trimmed and sliced, with strained fresh lemon juice (about 2 tablespoons) stirred into them. When assembling the salad, drain the mushrooms. Toss the salad with Vinaigrette Sauce, about ⅓ cup.

For 4 people, use 1 large bunch watercress.

Muffins

Yield: about 12 muffins
Preparation: about 10 minutes
Cooking: 20 minutes in a 400° F. oven
Doubles; refrigerates; freezes

2 cups flour
1 tablespoon baking powder
1 tablespoon sugar
¼ teaspoon salt

1. In a mixing bowl, sift together the dry ingredients and reserve them.

1 egg
1 cup milk
3 tablespoons cooking oil

2. In a mixing bowl, using a rotary beater, blend the liquid ingredients. Butter twelve muffin cups.

At this point you may stop and continue later. (Refrigerate the egg mixture, well covered; beat it briefly before continuing with the recipe.)

3. To the dry ingredients, add the liquid, stirring only to moisten the flour. Fill the prepared muffin cups two-thirds full. Bake the muffins at 400° F. for 20 minutes, or until they are well risen and golden.

Poached Pears with Raspberry Sauce

Yield: 4 servings
Preparation: about 15 minutes
Cooking: about 35 minutes
Doubles; refrigerates

½ cup sugar
½ cup ruby port wine
½ cup water
1 small lemon, sliced

1. In a flameproof casserole, combine the sugar, port wine, water, and lemon slices. Bring the mixture to the boil and cook it, uncovered, for 5 minutes.

4 large firm ripe pears (Anjou, Bosc, Comice), peeled, halved lengthwise, and cored

2. To the contents of the casserole, add the pears, spooning the syrup over them. Reduce the heat and poach the pears, covered, basting them frequently, for about 20 minutes, or until they are tender. With a slotted spoon, remove them to a serving bowl.

1 (10-ounce) package frozen raspberries, thawed

3. Over high heat, reduce the syrup to about one-half its volume. Add the raspberries and, over medium heat, cook the sauce, uncovered, for 5 minutes. Strain it over the pears, which may be served chilled or at room temperature.

Mushroom Rice with Saffron for 6

Mushroom Rice with Saffron
Green Bean Salad (page 4)
Fresh Fruit of Your Choice
Cookies of Your Choice

A day ahead:

complete step 1 of the rice recipe; prepare the ingredients of step 2

prepare the vinaigrette sauce and refrigerate it

cook the green beans

In the morning:

complete step 2 of the green bean salad recipe

Mushroom Rice with Saffron

Yield: 6 servings
Preparation: about 25 minutes
Cooking: 30 minutes
Doubles

4 tablespoons butter
1 pound mushrooms, trimmed and sliced
6 scallions, trimmed and chopped, with as much of the green as is crisp
1½ cups raw natural rice
Generous pinch of saffron

1. In a large saucepan or flameproof casserole, heat the butter and in it cook the mushrooms and scallions until they are limp. Add the rice, stirring to coat each grain. Stir in the saffron.

At this point you may stop and continue later.

2 cups chicken broth
1 cup dry white wine
½ cup chopped parsley
½ cup grated Parmesan cheese

2. To the contents of the saucepan, add the chicken broth and wine. Bring the liquid to the boil, reduce the heat, and simmer the rice, covered, for 15 minutes, or until it is tender and the liquid is absorbed.

Add the parsley and Parmesan cheese and, using two forks, gently toss the rice before transferring it to a heated dish. Serve it at once.

Fresh Fruit of Your Choice

Your choice, of course, depends upon the season of the year. Melon, sliced peaches, or pears go well, but you may also add a little "chic" to the meal by offering mango, papaya, or kiwi! How about pineapple with *Kirschwasser*?

Pasta with Sausage Sauce for 6

Pasta with Sausage Sauce
Lettuce, Watercress, and Red Onion Salad
(with Vinaigrette Sauce, page xxv)
Fresh Fruit and Cheese of Your Choice

A day or 2 ahead:

make steps 1, 2, and 3 of the sausage recipe

A day ahead:

prepare the salad ingredients and refrigerate them in separate plastic bags

prepare the vinaigrette sauce and refrigerate it

Pasta with Sausage Sauce

Yield: 6 servings
Preparation: about 30 minutes
Cooking: about 2 hours (but you do not have to stand guard)
Doubles: refrigerates

1 pound sweet Italian sausage meat

1. If in skin casings, remove the skin from the sausage, roll the meat into small balls and, in a large skillet, cook them, a few at a time, until they are crisp and brown. Drain them on absorbent paper and reserve them. Discard all but 3 tablespoons of the fat.

1 large rib celery, trimmed and chopped fine
2 cloves garlic, peeled and chopped
2 medium onions, peeled and chopped
1 (6-ounce) can tomato paste
1 (35-ounce) can crushed Italian tomatoes

2. In the fat, cook the celery, garlic, and onions until translucent. Stir in the tomato paste and tomatoes.

1 teaspoon basil
1 bay leaf
½ teaspoon marjoram
½ teaspoon thyme
2 teaspoons sugar
Reserved sausage balls
Salt, if desired
Fresh-ground pepper

3. Into the contents of the skillet, stir the first five seasonings and the sausage balls. Bring the mixture just to the boil, reduce the heat to low, and simmer the sauce, uncovered, for 1½ hours, or until it is thickened. Adjust the seasoning to taste with salt and pepper.

At this point you may stop and continue later. (Refrigerate the skillet, covered. Reheat the sauce when you are cooking the pasta.)

1½ pounds fettuccine, linguine, *or* spaghetti (the dish is especially good made with spinach pasta)
½ cup fine-chopped parsley

4. Cook and drain the pasta according to the directions on the package; do not overcook it. Transfer it to a large heated bowl and over it pour the sausage sauce; sprinkle over the parlsey. Using two forks, gently toss the mixture to blend it well. Serve it at once, accompanied by a well-filled pepper mill.

Lettuce, Watercress, and Red Onion Salad

For 4 servings, use 2 medium heads Boston lettuce and 1 large bunch watercress, both rinsed, spun dry, and the woody stems removed from the cress. Tear the leaves into bite-size pieces. Dress the salad with Vinaigrette Sauce, about 1/3 cup, and garnish it with 1 medium red onion, peeled, sliced thin, and separated into rings.

Fresh Fruit and Cheese of Your Choice

One of the tastiest and most satisfying of desserts! At our supermarkets, alas, the fruit one buys is usually unripe. The trick is to purchase fruit sufficiently ahead of time so that it is *à point* when you wish to serve it. Befriend a knowledgeable green-grocer who will be able to help with this problem.

Guaranteed combinations: apples and Cheddar, pears and blue cheese. Any bland, smooth cheese goes well with guava shells (available canned and very good). A macédoine of fruit is enhanced by a ripe Camembert or Brie (offer Melba toast to transport the cheese from plate to mouth). If you can get young Parmesan cheese (not yet rock-hard) it will melt in your mouth, literally and figuratively, accompanied by any fruit you care to serve.

A Two-Salad Lunch for 6

Greek Salad
French Potato Salad with Vinaigrette Sauce (page xxv)
Melon or Sherbet of Your Choice
Cookies of Your Choice, if desired

2 days ahead:

make the Vinaigrette Sauce

A day ahead:

cook and refrigerate the eggs but do not peel them

make the potato salad and the sauce; do not dress it until the next day

prepare the lettuce for the salad and refrigerate in a plastic bag

Greek Salad

Yield: 6 servings Refrigerates
Preparation: about 25 minutes

1 large head romaine lettuce, rinsed and dried on absorbent paper

1. On a large serving plate, arrange a bed of the romaine.

1 large cucumber, peeled and sliced
1 large red *or* 1 medium Spanish onion, peeled and sliced
1 medium green pepper, seeded, and cut in julienne strips
3 large ripe tomatoes, peeled and sliced
18 to 24 ripe olives (oil-cured olives are the most authentic)
1 pound feta cheese, cut in cubes
Sprinkling of oregano
Sprinkling of thyme
Strained juice of 1 large lemon (about 2½ tablespoons)
Fresh-ground pepper
Olive oil

2. On the romaine, arrange the first six ingredients. Season them to taste with oregano, thyme, lemon juice, and pepper. Over all, drizzle olive oil.

6 hard-cooked eggs, peeled and halved lengthwise
2 cans boneless sardines in oil, thoroughly drained
1 (14-ounce) can water-pack tuna, drained, and divided into 6 portions

3. Just before serving the salad, add to the arrangement the eggs, sardines, and tuna.

French Potato Salad

This potato salad is dressed with garlic vinaigrette and garnished with lots of parsley. I find it delicious and more unusual than the customary potato salad laced with mayonnaise.

Yield: 6 servings
Preparation: about 45 minutes (a day ahead, if you wish)
Chilling time: at least 3 hours prior to serving
Doubles: refrigerates (overnight)

1. To the Lemon Vinaigrette Sauce, add 3 large cloves garlic, peeled and put through a press. The garlic vinaigrette sauce will improve if made 1 or 2 days ahead and allowed to work.

Boiling water
6 medium boiling potatoes

2. In boiling water to cover, cook the potatoes for 20 minutes, or until they are fork tender; do not overcook them. Refresh them in cold water before peeling them; cut them into medium-size dice.

2 cups chopped parsley

3. In a large stainless steel or crockery bowl, combine the potatoes and parsley. Add sufficient vinaigrette sauce to coat the potatoes well as you toss them with the parsley. The salad should be moist but not runny. Chill it, covered, for at least 3 hours so that the flavors meld.

Melon or Sherbet of Your Choice

Cantaloupe! Serve ripe cantaloupe because it is most like the richer melon eaten in Greece. Or lemon sherbet, which is pleasantly tangy (with or without cookies of your choice).

Salmon Salad for 6

Salmon Salad
Ratatouille
Melba Toast
Strawberry Tart

2 days ahead:

hard-cook the eggs and refrigerate them but do not peel them

A day ahead:

prepare the vegetables and greens for the salad; refrigerate them, well covered with plastic wrap, separately

make the ratatouille

make the strawberry tart

An hour or 2 ahead:

complete the salad platter

Salmon Salad

If you prefer tuna fish salad, substitute 2 (7-ounce) cans of water-pack tuna for the salmon.

Yield: 6 servings
Preparation: about 25 minutes
Chilling time: at least 3 hours
Doubles; refrigerates (for a day or 2)

1 large rib celery, trimmed and diced
1 large cucumber, peeled, seeded, and diced
2 tablespoons fine-chopped dill pickle
2 scallions, trimmed and chopped fine, with some of the crisp green part
1 (16-ounce) can salmon, drained, the skin and bones removed

1. In a mixing bowl, combine these five ingredients. Using a fork, toss to blend them and to break up the salmon into small bits.

Mayonnaise (about ½ cup)
Strained fresh lemon juice
Fresh-ground white pepper

2. To the contents of the mixing bowl, add sufficient mayonnaise to bind the ingredients. Season the salmon salad to taste with lemon juice and pepper. Cover the bowl with plastic wrap and chill the salad for at least 3 hours.

3. Chill the serving platter for the salad.

Salad greens of your choice
3 *or* 6 hard-cooked eggs, peeled and halved lengthwise
Cherry tomatoes, stemmed and halved
Fine-chopped parsley

4. On the chilled serving platter, arrange the salad greens. Over them, in individual helpings, spoon the salad mixture. Garnish the platter with the egg halves, topped with a little mayonnaise, and cherry tomatoes. Sprinkle the salmon salad and egg halves with a little parsley. The platter may be arranged and kept, refrigerated, for up to 2 hours before serving.

Ratatouille

This recipe may be served hot or at room temperature (served chilled, it lacks flavor, I feel).

Yield: 6 servings
Preparation: about 30 minutes
Cooking: 45 minutes
Doubles; refrigerates
(a day ahead, if you wish)

⅓ cup olive oil
3 cloves garlic, peeled and chopped fine
2 medium onions, peeled and chopped

1. In a flameproof casserole, heat the olive oil and in it cook the garlic and onions until translucent.

¼ cup seasoned flour
1 medium eggplant, peeled and cubed
2 large zucchini, trimmed and sliced

2. In the seasoned flour, dredge the eggplant and zucchini; add them to the contents of the casserole.

2 medium green peppers, seeded and cut in strips
5 medium ripe tomatoes, peeled, seeded, and chopped coarse, *or*
1 (19-ounce) can tomatoes, with their liquid
Sprinkling of oregano *or* thyme
Strained juice of ½ medium lemon (about 1 tablespoon)
Salt, if desired
Fresh-ground pepper

3. Into the contents of the casserole, stir the remaining ingredients. Simmer the ratatouille, covered, for 15 minutes; remove the cover and continue to cook the ratatouille for 15 minutes longer, or until the vegetables are tender. The consistency should be moist but not soupy; continue to cook the ratatouille, uncovered, to evaporate excess liquid.

For flavor accents, add before cooking:

1 small head fennel, sliced
3 ribs celery, chopped coarse

Strawberry Tart

Yield: 6 servings (1 [8-inch] tart)
Preparation: 30 minutes (the time does not include readying pastry shells)
Chilling time: at least 3 hours
Refrigerates

1 (8-ounce) package cream cheese, at room temperature
¾ cup heavy cream
¼ cup orange-flavored liqueur
½ teaspoon vanilla
3 tablespoons sugar

1. In a mixing bowl, combine these five ingredients and blend them until the mixture is smooth.

1 (8-inch) pastry shell, baked, *or* graham-cracker crust (available ready-to-use at your supermarket)
1 quart strawberries, hulled, rinsed, and drained on absorbent paper

2. Spread the pie shell evenly with the cream cheese mixture. Over it, arrange the strawberries, standing on their stem ends.

1 (10-ounce) package frozen strawberries, fully thawed to room temperature
⅔ cup sugar
2 tablespoons cornstarch
2 teaspoons amaretto

3. In the container of a blender, whirl the thawed strawberries until the purée is smooth. Transfer it to a saucepan. Mix the sugar with the cornstarch and add it to the purée. Over moderate heat, cook the mixture, stirring constantly, until it is thickened and smooth. Stir in the amaretto. Allow the sauce to cool before spooning it over the strawberries in the tart. Chill the tart for at least 3 hours.

Creamed Chicken with Mushrooms for 4

Creamed Chicken with Mushrooms
Rice, page xx
Tomato Aspic with Watercress
Prunes in Port Wine

If you offer this simple but tasty meal as luncheon for 8 (the recipes double), you may want to make it more festive by using patty shells in place of rice and, for color on the plate, you might offer frozen small green peas. Prepared patty shells are readily available in the frozen foods case of your supermarket; bake them according to the directions on the package; to prepare the peas, follow the directions in the recipe below.

2 days ahead:

cook the prunes

make the tomato aspic

refrigerate the canned chicken broth

A day ahead:

prepare step 1 of the creamed chicken recipe

prepare the mushrooms and pimientos; refrigerate them separately, covered with plastic wrap

Creamed Chicken with Mushrooms

Yield: 4 servings
Preparation: about 40 minutes
Cooking: about 15 minutes
Doubles; refrigerates; freezes

1 large skinless, boneless chicken breast, trimmed of all fat
1 (10½-ounce) can chicken broth, defatted

1. In a saucepan, combine the chicken breast and broth. Bring the liquid to the boil, reduce the heat to low, and poach the chicken, covered, for about 10 minutes, or until it is fork tender. Away from the heat, allow it to cool in the broth. Cut the chicken into ½-inch cubes (you should have about 2 cups); strain the broth and reserve 1 cup.

At this point you may stop and continue later. (Refrigerate the cubed chicken, tightly covered; cover and refrigerate the broth.)

2 tablespoons butter
6 large mushrooms, trimmed and chopped coarse
2 tablespoons flour
¼ cup chopped canned pimientos
Salt, if desired
A few grains of cayenne pepper
Grating of nutmeg

2. In a saucepan, heat the butter and in it, over gentle heat, cook the mushrooms until they are limp. Stir in the flour and continue to cook the mixture for a few minutes. Gradually add the chicken broth, stirring constantly until the sauce is thickened and smooth. Stir in the chicken and pimientos. Season the mixture to taste.

1 egg
2 tablespoons heavy cream
1 tablespoon dry sherry, if desired

3. In a small mixing bowl, beat together the egg, cream, and sherry. Stir the mixture into the creamed chicken and bring it to serving temperature; do not allow it to boil.

Green Peas

Two (10-ounce) packages frozen small green peas will yield 4 generous servings. I am particularly partial to small peas—sometimes called "tiny" or "petite" on the package—for they require barely more than heating through to become tender. Cook the peas in unsalted water according to the timing on the package, bearing in mind that they cook very rapidly; do not overcook them. Drain and dress them with soft butter and white pepper, using a rubber spatula so that the peas do not squash.

If desired, you may prepare the peas fully a few hours ahead; heat them in the microwave oven for serving.

If you are preparing the recipe for 6 persons, use 3 (10-ounce) packages; for 8 persons, 4 packages are more than adequate.

For flavor accents, add to the peas:

a splash of white *crème de menthe* or Pernod, a little powdered dried mint, or a sprinkling of fresh lemon juice.

Tomato Aspic with Watercress

Yield: 4 servings
Preparation: about 15 minutes
Chilling time: at least 6 hours
Doubles; refrigerates

1 envelope unflavored gelatin
¾ teaspoon sugar
¾ cup canned tomato juice cocktail

1. In a saucepan, combine these three ingredients and, over moderate heat, stir the mixture until the gelatin is dissolved.

1 cup chilled tomato juice cocktail
½ cup chopped watercress leaves
Strained fresh lemon juice
A few drops of hot-pepper sauce
A few drops of Worcestershire sauce

2. Into the gelatin mixture, stir the chilled tomato juice cocktail (its being chilled will make the aspic gel more rapidly) and the watercress. Season the mixture to taste.

3. Into individual molds rinsed with cold water, pour the mixture. Chill the aspics for at least 6 hours, or until they are thoroughly set.

4 sprigs of watercress

4. To serve the aspics, dip the molds for about 5 seconds in warm (not hot) water and invert them onto individual chilled plates. Garnish each aspic with a sprig of watercress.

Stewed Prunes

Yield: 4 generous servings (you will probably have enough for 2 meals)
Preparation: about 5 minutes
Cooking: about 20 minutes
Chilling time: at least 3 hours
Doubles; refrigerates

1 (11-ounce) package tenderized pitted prunes
3 slices lemon
3 tablespoons sugar
Water to cover

In a saucepan, arrange the prunes and lemon slices; sprinkle them with the sugar. Add water just to cover. Bring the liquid to the boil, reduce the heat, and simmer the prunes, covered, for 20 minutes, or until they are tender. Remove the cover and allow them to cool in the liquid before chilling them for at least 3 hours.

FOR VARIATION:
Stewed Apricots: Follow the recipe for Stewed Prunes but substitute 1 (11-ounce) package tenderized pitted dried apricots for the prunes.

Prunes in Port Wine

Follow the directions for Stewed Prunes, above, using ruby port in place of the water and adding the zest of 1 orange together with the lemon slices. If desired, offer sour cream as a topping for the prunes.

Curried Shrimp for 4

Curried Shrimp
Rice (see page xx)
Mango Chutney
Baked Cherry Tomatoes
Melon with Port Wine

(Menu Halves)

A day ahead:

prepare step 1 of the cherry tomato recipe; refrigerate them, well covered

prepare the melon

refrigerate the canned chicken broth

A few hours ahead:

thaw the shrimp in tepid water; drain them well; refrigerate them if necessary, until you are ready to proceed with the recipe

Curried Shrimp

Yield: 4 servings
Preparation: about 30 minutes
Cooking: about 20 minutes
Doubles

1 (1-pound) package shelled and cooked frozen shrimp, fully thawed to room temperature and drained; *or* 1 pound fresh shrimp, peeled and cooked (see page 21)
4 tablespoons butter
1 large clove garlic, peeled and chopped fame
1 medium onion, peeled and chopped
4 tablespoons flour

1. In a saucepan, heat the butter and in it cook the garlic and onion until translucent. Stir in the flour and, over gentle heat, cook the mixture for a few minutes.

1½ teaspoons (or to taste) curry powder
¼ teaspoon ground ginger
2 cups defatted canned chicken broth
1 cup light cream
Grated rind of 1 medium lemon
2 tablespoons strained fresh lemon juice

2. Into the contents of the saucepan, stir the curry powder and the ginger. Gradually add the chicken broth and then the cream, stirring constantly until the mixture is thickened and smooth. Stir in the lemon rind and juice.

3. To the sauce, add the shrimp and heat them through.

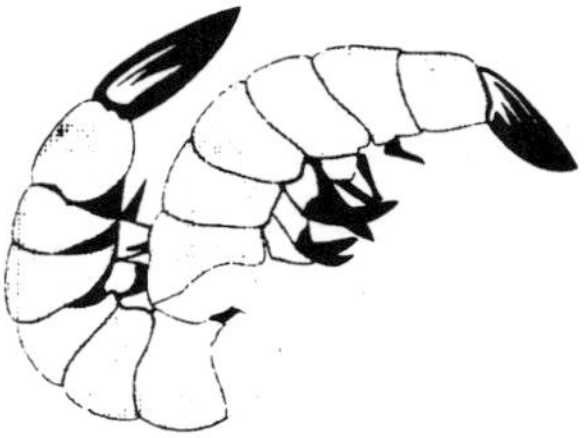

Baked Cherry Tomatoes

Yield: 4 servings
Preparation: about 12 minutes

Cooking: about 6 minutes in a 400° F. oven
Doubles

3 tablespoons butter
Grated rind of 1 medium lemon
Fresh-ground pepper
16 to 20 firm ripe cherry tomatoes, their stems removed, rinsed, and dried on absorbent paper

1. In a large saucepan, melt the butter; add the lemon rind and a generous grinding of pepper. Add the cherry tomatoes and, using a rubber spatula, gently toss them to coat them well. Arrange them in a single layer in an ovenproof serving dish; add to them any remaining butter.

At this point you may stop and continue later. (Refrigerate the tomatoes well covered.)

Fine-chopped parsley

2. Bake the tomatoes, uncovered, in a 400° F. oven for about 6 minutes. Garnish the dish with parsley.

If you are preparing this dish to serve 6 persons, use 24 to 30 cherry tomatoes and 4 tablespoons butter.

Melon with Port Wine

Yield: 4 servings
Preparation: about 5 minutes
Chilling time: at least 6 hours or overnight

1 large ripe cantaloupe *or* other melon
Port wine (ruby or white, depending on the color of the melon)

1. With a sharp-pointed knife, cut a plug from the stem end of the melon. Shake out as many seeds as possible. With the wine, fill the cavity of the melon, replace the plug, and refrigerate the fruit, supported so that it will stand, for at least 6 hours.

2. To serve the melon, pour off and reserve the wine. Quarter the melon lengthwise, remove the remaining seeds, and over each slice spoon some of the reserved wine.

If you are preparing this recipe for 6 persons, use 2 medium melons.

Salmon Steaks with Orange-Saffron Sauce for 4

Salmon Steaks with Orange-Saffron Sauce
Green Peas, page 47
Braised Belgian Endive
Lime Sherbet
Cookies of Your Choice

(Menu Halves)

I first enjoyed salmon steaks cooked this way at an excellent hillside village restaurant outside Bayreuth, Germany, where I had gone for the Wagner festival. It is quite an elegant dish and serves well as party fare.

A day ahead:
refrigerate the canned chicken broth

Several hours ahead, if desired:
prepare the green peas

Salmon Steaks with Orange-Saffron Sauce

Yield: 4 servings
Preparation: about 15 minutes
Cooking: 15 minutes

Strained juice of ½ medium lemon
1½ cups strained fresh orange juice
Grated rind of 1 medium orange
½ cup dry white wine
4 salmon steaks (⅓ to ½ pound each—ask your fishmonger for steaks of equal size, each to yield 1 serving)

1. In a skillet large enough to accommodate the salmon steaks in a single layer, combine and bring to the boil the lemon and orange juices, orange rind, and wine. Add the salmon steaks and poach them without turning them for about 10 minutes, or until they flake easily. Remove them to a heated serving platter and keep them warm while you prepare the sauce.

Large pinch of saffron
¼ cup heavy cream
2 egg yolks, beaten
Salt, if desired
Fresh-ground white pepper
¼ cup fine-chopped parsley

2. Into the contents of the skillet, crumble the saffron. Over gentle heat, stir in the cream and then the egg yolks. Stir the sauce constantly until it is somewhat thickened and smooth; do not allow it to boil. Season it to taste. Spoon the sauce over the salmon steaks and garnish them with parsley.

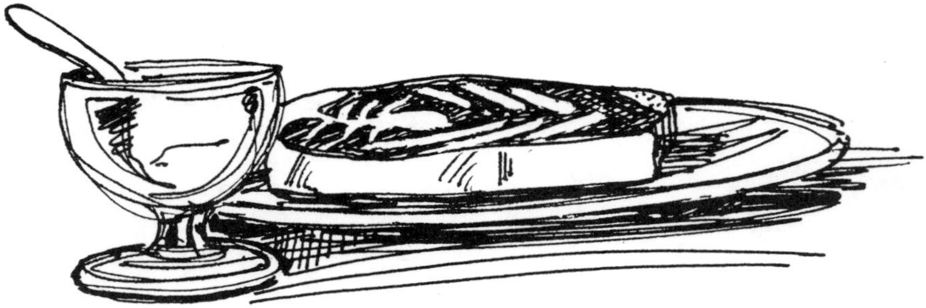

Braised Belgian Endive

Yield: 4 servings
Preparation: about 5 minutes
Cooking: 20 minutes
Doubles

4 large Belgian endives, trimmed and split lengthwise
½ cup dry white wine
½ cup defatted canned chicken broth
Butter

In a large skillet with a cover, arrange the endives, split side up. Over them, pour the wine and chicken broth. Dot them with butter. Over high heat, bring the liquid to the boil, reduce the heat, and simmer the vegetable, covered, for 10 minutes. Increase the heat to medium high, turn the endives over, and continue to cook them, uncovered, for 10 minutes, or until they are tender and the liquid thickens somewhat.Offer them on separate plates from the salmon.

Veal Scallops Marsala for 4

Veal Scallops Marsala
Rice with Mushrooms
Bibb Lettuce Salad with Vinaigrette Sauce (page xxv)
Pineapple in Orange Syrup

(Menu Halves)

A day ahead:

prepare the vegetables for the rice with mushrooms and refrigerate them

prepare the lettuce and refrigerate it in a plastic bag

prepare the vinaigrette sauce and refrigerate it

prepare the pineapple and refrigerate it

Veal Scallops Marsala

Yield: 4 servings
Preparation: about 15 minutes
Cooking: about 15 minutes
Doubles

4 veal scallops, cut ½ inch thick (about 1½ pounds total)

1. With a meat mallet or heavy knife, pound the scallops until they are about ¼ inch thick.

Seasoned flour
3 tablespoons butter
1 tablespoon oil

2. In the seasoned flour, dust the scallops; shake off any excess flour. In a skillet, over medium-high heat, heat the butter and oil and sauté the scallops for 3 minutes per side. Remove them to a heated serving platter and keep them warm while you prepare the sauce.

¼ cup defatted canned chicken broth
¼ cup dry Marsala
1 tablespoon soft butter
Fine-chopped parsley

3. Over high heat, deglaze the skillet with the chicken broth and Marsala. When the sauce thickens slightly, stir in the butter. Pour the sauce over the scallops and garnish the dish with parsley.

Rice with Mushrooms

Yield: 4 servings
Preparation: about 15 minutes
Cooking: 20 minutes
Doubles

- **½ cup fine-chopped celery**
- **½ pound mushrooms, sliced**
- **1 small onion, peeled and chopped fine**

1. If you prepare the celery, mushrooms, and onion a day ahead, cover them with plastic wrap and refrigerate them.

- **2 tablespoons butter**
- **1 cup raw natural rice**
- **¼ teaspoon thyme**
- **1⅔ cups defatted canned chicken broth**
- **⅓ cup dry white wine**

2. In a saucepan, over medium-high heat, melt the butter and in it cook the celery, mushrooms, and onion until the onion is translucent. Add the rice, stirring to coat each grain. Stir in the thyme. Add the chicken broth and wine. Bring the liquid to the boil, stir the mixture once with a fork, reduce the heat, and simmer the rice, covered, for 15 minutes, or until it is tender and the liquid is absorbed.

Bibb Lettuce Salad

Use 2 medium heads Bibb lettuce for 4 servings. If you cannot find Bibb lettuce, use any tender leaf lettuce that looks fresh and crisp. Rinse and spin dry the leaves. Tear them into bite-size pieces. Dress the salad with Vinaigrette Sauce, about ⅓ cup.

If you are preparing this salad for 6 persons, use 3 medium heads Bibb lettuce.

Pineapple in Orange Syrup

Yield: 4 servings
Preparation: about 20 minutes
Chilling time: 3 hours
Doubles; refrigerates

1 ripe pineapple (about 2 pounds)

1. With a sharp knife, cut off the ends of the pineapple. Cut the pineapple in lengthwise halves, then in quarters, and finally in eighths. Cut the rind from each section; cut away and discard the core (you will be able to distinguish it from the flesh of the fruit by its texture and slightly different color); cut out any black eyes that may have remained from removing the rind. Last, cut the sections into bite-size pieces and reserve them.

Zest of 1 large orange, cut in fine julienne
1½ cups strained fresh orange juice
1½ cups sugar
A few grains of salt
⅓ cup orange-flavored liqueur

2. In a saucepan, combine the orange zest and juice, the sugar, and salt. Over high heat, bring the liquid to the boil, stirring to dissolve the sugar. Boil the mixture, uncovered, for about 5 minutes, or until it is slightly syrupy. Stir in the liqueur.

Reserved pineapple

3. To the hot syrup, add the pineapple and continue to cook the dessert, uncovered, for 5 minutes. Allow it to cool somewhat before transferring it to a serving bowl. Chill it, well covered, for at least 3 hours or overnight

If you are preparing this recipe for 6 or 8 persons, use a large pineapple (about 3 pounds). In any case, there will probably be some left over, and for that reason I do not alter ingredient quantities for the syrup.

Chicken Livers and Mushrooms for 4

Chicken Livers and Mushrooms
Rice, page xx, or Toasted English Muffins
Broccoli
Compote of Fresh Plums

(Menu Halves)

A day ahead:

prepare the chicken livers for soaking and refrigerate them

prepare the mushrooms

make the fresh plum compote; refrigerate it

A few hours ahead:

in a bowl, soak the chicken livers in lightly salted water

Chicken Livers and Mushrooms

Yield: 4 servings
Preparation: about 20 minutes (the time does not include soaking the livers)
Cooking: about 12 minutes
Doubles

Seasoned flour
1 pound chicken livers, halved, any membrane or fat removed; soaked for several hours in salted water, refrigerated, drained, and dried on absorbent paper
2 tablespoons butter
2 tablespoons oil

1. In the seasoned flour, dredge the chicken livers; shake off any excess flour and reserve it. In a skillet, heat the butter and oil and, over medium-high heat, sauté the chicken livers for about 2 minutes per side, or until they are slightly golden. Remove and reserve them.

Butter
1 medium onion, peeled and chopped fine
½ pound button mushrooms, quartered (*or* larger mushrooooms, sliced)

2. In the skillet, heat a little more butter if necessary; add the onion and mushrooms and cook them, stirring, until the mushrooms are limp.

1 tablespoon reserved seasoned flour
½ cup dry Madeira, Marsala, or sherry
Reserved chicken livers
Fine-chopped parsley

3. Into the mushrooms, stir the reserved seasoned flour. Add the wine of your choice and, over medium-high heat, cook the mixture, stirring gently, until the sauce is thickened. Reduce the heat. Gently stir in the chicken livers and simmer the dish, covered, for 2 minutes, or until the livers are heated through; do not overcook them. Garnish them with parsley. Prepared this way, chicken livers are especially good with rice, but are equally tasty if you prefer to serve them on buttered toasted English muffins.

Broccoli

Two (10-ounce) packages frozen broccoli spears will yield 4 servings. Cook them according to the directions on the package; do not overcook them. Dress the broccoli spears with soft butter and fresh lemon juice.

If you are preparing this for 6 to 8 persons, allow 3 (10-ounce) packages frozen broccoli spears.

Compote of Fresh Plums

Yield: 4 servings
Preparation: about 15 minutes
Cooking: 10 minutes
Chilling time: at least 3 hours
Doubles; refrigerates

⅓ cup sugar
1 cup dry red wine
1 cup strained fresh orange juice
4 cloves
1 (3-inch) piece cinnamon stick
Zest of 1 lemon
A few grains of salt, if desired

1. In a saucepan, combine these ingredients. Over high heat bring the liquid to a rolling boil and cook the mixture, uncovered, for 5 minutes.

16 firm, ripe purple or red plums, rinsed, and pricked in several places with a toothpick (to prevent their skins from bursting)

2. To the syrup, add the plums. When the syrup returns to the boil, reduce the heat and simmer the plums for 5 minutes. Cool and then chill the plums in the syrup for at least 3 hours.

Potato Soup for 6

Potato Soup
French Bread
Green Bean Salad
Cheese Tray of Your Choice
Sherbet of Your Choice

A day ahead:

make the soup

prepare step 1 of the bean salad

prepare the lemon vinaigrette sauce and refrigerate it

Several hours ahead:

dress the green bean salad

Potato Soup

Yield: 6 to 8 servings
Preparation and cooking: about 1 hour

Doubles; refrigerates; freezes

3 tablespoons butter
1 medium carrot, scraped and chopped
1 large rib celery, chopped
3 large leeks, rinsed and chopped, the white part only

1. In a soup kettle, heat the butter and in it cook the vegetables until the leeks are limp.

5 medium potatoes, peeled and chopped
***Bouquet garni* (page xiii)**
5 (10½-ounce) cans defatted chicken broth

2. To the vegetables, add the potatoes, *bouquet garni*, and chicken broth. Bring the liquid to the boil, reduce the heat, and simmer the potatoes, covered, for 30 minutes, or until they are very tender.

3. Allow the mixture to cool somewhat. Remove and discard the *bouquet garni*. In the container of a food processor or blender, whirl the soup, about 2 cups at a time, until it is smooth. Transfer it to a large saucepan.

1 cup light cream
Salt, if desired
Fresh-ground white pepper
Soft butter

4. Into the soup, stir the cream; season it to taste with salt and pepper. In each of six soup bowls, put a dollop of soft butter. Heat the soup back to serving temperature, but do not boil it, and ladle it over the butter.

French Bread

Purchase the best quality possible. Heat it briefly in a hot oven to crisp the crust, and offer it with sweet butter.

Green Bean Salad

Yield: 6 servings
Preparation: about 20 minutes
Cooking: 20 minutes
Chilling time: at least 3 hours

1½ pounds fresh green beans, the ends trimmed, cut in half, and rinsed in cold water
About 6 quarts water

1. In a soup kettle, bring to a rolling boil about 6 quarts of water. Add the beans, allow the water to return to the boil, and cook them, uncovered, for about 8 minutes, or until they are tender-crisp. Refresh them at once in cold water and thoroughly drain them.

At this point you may stop and continue later. (Refrigerate the beans. covered.)

About ⅓ cup Lemon Vinaigrette Sauce (page xxv)
Fine-chopped parsley

2. In a large bowl, toss the beans with the sauce, enough to coat them well. Garnish the salad with parsley and chill it for at least 3 hours so that the flavors meld.

Cheese Tray of Your Choice

A soft-ripening cheese (such as Brie, Camembert, or Caprice des Dieux); a semi-hard cheese (such as Pont l'Evêque); a goat cheese; and a blue cheese (such as Bleu d'Auvergne, Roquefort, or Bleu de Bresse).

Oyster Stew for 4

Oyster Stew
Muffins, page 35
Spinach and Mushroom Salad with Vinaigrette Sauce (page xxv)
Compote of Fresh Plums, page 59

(Menu Halves)

A day ahead:

measure and combine the dry and liquid ingredients for the muffins; refrigerate the liquid

make the fresh plum compote and refrigerate it

prepare step 1 and step 2 of spinach salad

prepare the vinaigrette sauce and refrigerate it

Oyster Stew

Yield: 4 servings

Preparation and cooking: about 20 minutes

3 tablespoons butter
1 small onion, peeled and grated
½ teaspoon celery salt
4 tablespoons flour
3 cups light cream

1. In a large saucepan, heat the butter and in it cook the onion for a few minutes; stir in the celery salt and flour and continue to cook the mixture for a few minutes. Gradually add the cream, stirring constantly until the mixture is slightly thickened and smooth.

1 quart shucked oysters, with their liquid
Salt, if desired
Fresh-ground white pepper

2. To the contents of the saucepan, add the oysters and their liquid. Over medium-high heat, cook the oysters until their edges begin to curl, about 4 minutes. Season the oyster stew to taste.

Spinach and Mushroom Salad

Yield: 4 servings Preparation: about 20 minutes

½ pound fresh spinach, the woody stems removed, rinsed in cold water and thoroughly drained

1. Cut or tear the spinach leaves into manageable size; refrigerate them in a plastic bag until you are ready to use them.

12 large white mushrooms, sliced
Strained juice of 1 lemon (about 2 tablespoons)

2. In a mixing bowl, fold together the mushrooms and lemon juice, so that the vegetable is well coated (this step will prevent the mushrooms from darkening). Discard any excess lemon juice.

About 1/3 cup Vinaigrette Sauce

3. At the time of serving, combine the spinach and mushrooms in a large bowl and dress them with vinaigrette sauce.

French Onion Soup for 6

French Onion Soup
French Bread
Green Salad with Vinaigrette Sauce (page xxv)
Fresh Fruit and Cheese of Your Choice, page 40

A day ahead:

prepare steps 1, 2, and 3 of the soup recipe

prepare the lettuce and watercress and refrigerate them in separate plastic bags

prepare the vinaigrette sauce and refrigerate it

grate the cheese for the soup and refrigerate it

French Onion Soup

Yield: 6 generous servings

Preparation and cooking: 30 minutes

3 tablespoons butter
3 tablespoons olive oil
6 large yellow onions, peeled and sliced thin

1. In a soup kettle, heat the butter and olive oil and in the mixture cook the onions until they are soft.

1 teaspoon sugar
3 tablespoons flour

2. Sprinkle the sugar over and continue to cook the onions, stirring, until they are golden. Stir in the flour and, over gentle heat, cook the mixture for a few minutes.

6 (10½-ounce) cans beef bouillon
1 cup dry red wine

3. Add the bouillon and wine. Bring the mixture to the boil, reduce the heat, and simmer the onions, covered, for 10 minutes.

At this point you may stop and continue later. (Refrigerate the soup kettle and its contents, covered.)

6 thick slices French bread
¾ cup grated Gruyère cheese
¾ cup grated Parmesan cheese

4. In a 350° F. oven, toast the bread slices until they are dry. Blend the two cheeses. Bring the soup to serving temperature.

5. To serve the soup, place a piece of bread in each plate; over the bread, sprinkle 2 or 3 tablespoons of the blended cheeses. Ladle the soup over the bread.

Green Salad

For 6 servings, combine 2 large heads leaf lettuce with 1 bunch watercress, the lettuce and cress rinsed and thoroughly spun dry, and the woody stems of the cress discarded. Tear the lettuce into bite-size pieces. Dress the salad with Vinaigrette Sauce, about ⅓ cup.

Scallops Provençale for 4

Scallops Provençale
Bulgur, page xx
Fresh Spinach with Mushrooms
Grapefruit with Amaretto

(Menu Halves)

A day ahead:

prepare step 1 of the scallop recipe

prepare the spinach, cover it with plastic wrap, and refrigerate it

prepare the mushrooms

A few hours ahead:

halve and section the grapefruit; over the sections, pour a little amaretto; refrigerate them, covered with plastic wrap

Scallops Provençale

Yield: 4 servings
Preparation: about 10 minutes
Cooking: about 8 minutes in a 400° F. oven
Doubles

4 tablespoons butter
4 cloves garlic, peeled and chopped fine
1 pound bay scallops *or* sea scallops, halved

1. In a saucepan, heat the butter and in it cook the garlic for 1 minute. Off the heat, add the scallops and, using a rubber spatula, fold them with the butter to coat them well. Transfer them and the butter to an ovenproof serving dish.

At this point you may stop and continue later. (Refrigerate the scallops, covered.)

Fine-chopped parsley
Lemon wedges

2. Bake the scallops at 400° F. for about 8 minutes, or until they are tender; do not overcook them. Garnish the dish with parsley and lemon wedges.

Fresh Spinach with Mushrooms

Yield: 4 servings
Preparation: about 15 minutes
Cooking: about 5 minutes
Doubles

4 tablespoons butter
2 scallions, trimmed and chopped fine, the white part only
½ pound mushrooms, sliced

1. In a large skillet or other utensil (a Chinese wok is admirable for this procedure), heat the butter and in it cook the scallions until they are limp. Add the mushrooms and toss them with the butter until they are slightly wilted.

2 (10-ounce) packages fresh leaf spinach, the woody stems removed, rinsed and thoroughly drained

2. To the contents of the utensil, add the spinach and, using two wooden spoons, toss it with the mushrooms until it is wilted.

If you are preparing this recipe for 6 persons, use 3 (10-ounce) packages fresh spinach.

Grapefruit with Amaretto

To serve 4 persons, halve 2 large grapefruit, cut out the centers, and section them with a grapefruit or other sharp-pointed knife; seed them. Into the cavities, pour amaretto. Arrange the grapefruit halves on a plate, cover them with plastic wrap, and refrigerate them.

Chicken Breasts with Vegetables for 4

Chicken Breasts with Vegetables with Mustard Sauce (page xix)
Rice, page xx
Melon with Port Wine, page 51
(Menu Halves)

A day ahead:

prepare the chicken breasts for cooking and refrigerate them covered with plastic wrap

prepare the vegetables and refrigerate them in water to cover

prepare the mustard sauce

prepare the melon

refrigerate the canned chicken broth

Chicken Breasts with Vegetables

Yield: 4 servings
Preparation: about 30 minutes
Cooking: about 15 minutes

4 medium carrots, scraped and cut in 1/8-inch rounds
1 large parsnip, scraped, quartered lengthwise, and cut in ½-inch pieces
12 to 16 Brussels sprouts, trimmed
1 large white turnip, scraped and cut in ½-inch dice
3 (10½-ounce) cans chicken broth, defatted
1 tablespoon strained fresh lemon juice

1. In a flameproof baking pan (that will accommodate the chicken breasts in a single layer) combine the vegetables, chicken broth, and lemon juice. Over high heat, bring the liquid to the boil; reduce the heat somewhat and cook the vegetables, covered (use foil wrap, if necessary), for about 6 minutes, or until the carrots and turnips are tender.

2 large full skinless, boneless chicken breasts, trimmed of all fat, and halved lengthwise (if large breasts are unavailable, allow 1 small breast per serving)
2 bunches scallions, trimmed and cut in 1-inch lengths, with only a little of the green part

2. In the pan, arrange the chicken in a single layer. Add the scallions. Over medium heat, cook the chicken, covered, for 7 minutes, turning it once; do not overcook it. With a slotted spoon, remove the breasts to heated dinner plates; surround them with the vegetables. Strain the broth and reserve it for use in a soup or sauce.

1 recipe Mustard Sauce
Fine-chopped parsley

3. Over the chicken, spoon some of the sauce; offer any remaining sauce separately. Garnish each serving with parsley.

Sautéed Calf's Liver for 4

Sautéed Calf's Liver
Baked Acorn Squash
Mixed Salad with Vinaigrette Sauce (page xxv)
Vanilla Ice Cream with Marmalade or Preserves
Cookies of Your Choice, if desired

(Menu Halves)

You will note that, although the sautéed liver is the first item on the menu, its preparation is a last-minute operation to be started only when the entire meal is ready.

A day ahead:

prepare the salad ingredients and refrigerate them in separate plastic bags

prepare the vinaigrette sauce and refrigerate it

prepare the preserves or marmalade syrup and refrigerate it

A few hours ahead:

prepare the acorn squash for cooking and refrigerate it

Sautéed Calf's Liver

Yield: 4 servings
Preparation: about 5 minutes
Cooking: about 5 minutes
Doubles

Seasoned flour
4 (¼-inch) slices calf's liver (about 1¼ to 1½ pounds)
4 tablespoons butter
Fine-chopped parsley
Lemon wedges

With seasoned flour, dust both sides of the liver slices. In a skillet, heat the butter until it is hot (do not allow it to darken); in it, sauté the liver, about 2 minutes per side; do not overcook it. Transfer the slices to warmed dinner plates and garnish them with parsley and a lemon wedge.

Baked Acorn Squash

Yield: 4 servings
Preparation: about 5 minutes
Cooking: 40 minutes in a 400° F. oven
Doubles

2 acorn squash of equal size, sliced lengthwise, the seeds removed
6 tablespoons butter
Dark rum, Bourbon whiskey, maple syrup, *or* dark brown sugar

In the cavity of each squash half, arrange 1½ tablespoons butter, then add rum, whiskey, syrup, or brown sugar to fill the cavity about two-thirds full. Arrange the squash on an ungreased baking sheet and cook them in a 400° F. oven for 40 minutes, or until they are fork tender. When serving the squash, offer additional butter.

Mixed Salad

For 4 servings, choose 2 heads different lettuces. Rinse and spin dry the leaves. Tear them into bite-size pieces. To them add a few cherry tomatoes, halved, some scallions, trimmed and chopped, and some water chestnuts, sliced (which give a nice crunch). Dress the salad with Vinaigrette Sauce, about ⅓ cup.

Vanilla Ice Cream with Marmalade or Preserves

Add sufficient hot water to the marmalade or preserves of your choice, stirring until the mixture spoons easily and is the consistency of thick syrup. Over scoops of ice cream, spoon a generous dollop of the syrup. (You will want an 8-ounce jar of marmalade or preserves.) For a more piquant accompaniment, I recommend either ginger preserves or bitter-orange marmalade. Offer the dessert with cookies of your choice, if desired.

Pasta for 4

Fettuccine in Parmesan Cream
Mixed Salad with Vinaigrette Sauce (page xxv)
Dried-Fruit Compote (page 19) or Chilled Zabaglione

A day ahead:

prepare step 1 of the fettuccine recipe

prepare the salad ingredients and refrigerate them in separate plastic bags

prepare the vinaigrette sauce and refrigerate it

make the fruit compote, if desired

On the day itself:

make the zabaglione, if desired

Fettuccine in Parmesan Cream

Yield: 4 servings
Preparation: about 10 minutes for the sauce; about 8 minutes for the pasta

Doubles

8 tablespoons butter
1 clove garlic, peeled and chopped fine
Grating of nutmeg
½ teaspoon salt, if desired
Generous grinding of white pepper
1 cup heavy cream (if desired, you may use light cream)
1 cup grated Parmesan cheese

1. In the top of a double boiler melt the butter and in it briefly cook the garlic. Add the nutmeg, salt, and pepper. Add the cream and Parmesan cheese and, over medium heat, cook the sauce, stirring, until the cheese melts and the mixture is somewhat thickened. Cover the sauce and reserve it.

At this point you may stop and continue later. (Refrigerate the sauce.)

1 (12-ounce) package fettuccine (I prefer spinach fettuccine not only nutritionally, but also visually—the green pasta and cream-colored sauce make an eye-appealing dish)
About 8 quarts boiling salted water

2. In a soup kettle, bring to the boil the salted water and in it cook the pasta according to the directions on the package; take care not to overcook it.

Reserved sauce

3. While the pasta is cooking, bring the sauce to serving temperature over simmering water or in the microwave oven. When the pasta is *al dente*, drain it and toss it with the heated sauce (a wok is an ideal utensil for this purpose). Divide the pasta among four warmed plates and serve it, accompanied by a pepper mill.

Mixed Salad

For 4 servings, choose 2 heads different lettuces. Rinse and spin dry the leaves. Tear them into bite-size pieces. To them add a few cherry tomatoes, halved, some scallions, trimmed and chopped, and some water chestnuts, sliced (which give a nice crunch). Dress the salad with Vinaigrette Sauce, about 1/3 cup.

Alternative Mixed Salad

Follow the directions in the recipe but omit the water chestnuts; to the salad, add sliced radishes and a few pitted ripe olives, rinsed and halved lengthwise. Dress the salad as directed.

Chilled Zabaglione

Yield: 4 servings

Chilling time: at least 3 hours
Refrigerates

1. Chill four parfait or other similar glasses.

6 egg yolks
6 tablespoons fine-granulated sugar
A few grains of salt, if desired
2/3 cup Marsala

2. In the top of a double boiler, using a rotary beater, beat the egg yolks while gradually adding first the sugar and salt and then the Marsala. Over boiling water, beat the mixture vigorously until it foams and is somewhat thickened; take care not to overcook the custard (it will curdle) and do not allow the boiling water to touch the top of the double boiler.

1/3 cup heavy cream, whipped

3. Place the top of the double boiler in a bowl of ice water and continue to beat the mixture until it is thoroughly cooled. Fold in the whipped cream. Using a rubber spatula, transfer the zabaglione to the prepared glasses and chill it for at least 3 hours.

Salmon Kedgeree for 6

Salmon Kedgeree
Mixed Salad with Vinaigrette Sauce (page xxv)
Pineapple with Kirschwasser

A day ahead:

prepare the salad ingredients and refrigerate them in separate plastic bags

prepare the vinaigrette sauce and refrigerate it

prepare the pineapple

Several hours ahead:

prepare steps 1, 2, and 3 of the kedgeree recipe

Salmon Kedgeree

Yield: 6 servings Doubles
Preparation: about 40 minutes

6 tablespoons butter
1 medium onion, peeled and chopped fine
1½ cups raw natural rice

1. In a large saucepan, heat the butter and in it cook the onion until translucent. Add the rice, stirring to coat each grain. Reserve the mixture.

1½ pounds fresh salmon fillet
3 cups strained fresh orange juice

2. In a skillet, bring the orange juice to simmer, add the fish, and poach it for about 10 minutes, or until it flakes easily. With a slotted spoon, remove the fish; flake it. Strain the orange juice and add it to the rice. Return the orange juice to boil, reduce the heat, and simmer the rice, covered, for 15 minutes, or until it is tender and the liquid is absorbed.

Strained juice of 1 small lemon (about 1½ tablespoons)
4 hard-cooked eggs, shelled, the whites chopped coarse and the yolks forced through a sieve
½ cup fine-chopped watercress leaves

3. In a large mixing bowl, using two forks, lightly toss together the cooked rice, flaked salmon, lemon juice, egg white, and watercress leaves. Adjust the seasoning to taste. Into a buttered ovenproof serving dish with a cover (or use aluminum foil), spoon the kedgeree.

At this point you may stop and continue later. (If you are planning to serve the kedgeree within a few hours, there is no need to refrigerate it; the cooked ingredients will hold well. If several hours will elapse between making the dish and serving it, refrigerate it, closely covered.)

4. To serve, heat the kedgeree in a 350° F. oven for about 20 minutes, or until it is of proper serving temperature; or heat it in the microwave oven.

Light cream, warmed
Reserved sieved egg yolk

5. Over the kedgeree, sprinkle a little cream to assure the moistness of the dish. Garnish the dish with the egg yolk.

Mixed Salad, Vinaigrette

For 6 servings, use 3 heads Bibb or 2 medium heads Boston lettuce; rinse and spin dry the leaves. Tear them into bite-size pieces. Add a few halved cherry tomatoes, some sliced cucumber, a few sliced mushrooms, and a few chopped scallions. Dress the salad with Vinaigrette Sauce, about 1/3 cup. Serve the salad as a side dish to the kedgeree.

If you are preparing the salad for 8 persons, use 4 heads Bibb or 2 large heads Boston lettuce.

Pineapple with Kirschwasser

For 6 servings, use a ripe pineapple that weighs about 3 pounds. To cut it, follow the directions on page 11. If desired, add to it a light dusting of powdered ginger. Toss the pineapple with 1/3 cup *Kirschwasser*. Transfer it to a serving bowl and refrigerate it, covered, for several hours.

Scallop Stew for 4

Scallop Stew
Cream Biscuits, page 15
Mixed Vegetable Salad, page 7
Dried-Fruit Compote, page 19

A day ahead:

complete step 1 of the stew recipe

complete step 1 of the biscuit recipe

prepare and refrigerate the vegetable salad

make the dried-fruit compote

Scallop Stew

Yield: 4 servings Doubles
Preparation and cooking: about 15 minutes

4 tablespoons butter
1 small onion, peeled and grated
¾ teaspoon celery salt
Fresh-ground white pepper
4 tablespoons flour
4 cups milk *or* light cream

1. In a saucepan, heat the butter and in it, over moderate heat, cook the onion and seasonings briefly. Stir in the flour and continue to cook the mixture for a few minutes. Gradually add the milk or cream, stirring constantly until the mixture is slightly thickened and smooth.

At this point you may stop and continue later. (Refrigerate the stew base, covered.)

1 pound bay scallops *or* sea scallops (you may want to halve or quarter large sea scallops)
Worcestershire sauce

2. Bring the milk mixture just to the boil; add the scallops. Over medium heat, barely simmer the scallops for 3 or 4 minutes, or until they are just firm; do not overcook them (they will become rubbery). Add a dash of Worcestershire sauce and serve the stew.

Crabmeat Florentine for 6

Crabmeat Florentine
Wild Rice
Baked Pears

2 days ahead:

refrigerate the canned chicken broth

bake the pears

A day ahead:

complete steps 1 and 2 of the crabmeat recipe

A few hours ahead:

prepare the wild rice for reheating at time of serving

Crabmeat Florentine

Yield: 6 servings Preparation: about 30 minutes

4 tablespoons butter
4 tablespoons flour
2 tablespoons cornstarch
1 cup canned chicken broth, defatted
1 cup milk
½ cup grated Swiss cheese
2 teaspoons fresh lemon juice
1 teaspoon Worcestershire sauce
A few drops of hot-pepper sauce

1. In the top of a double boiler, over direct medium heat, melt the butter and in it cook the flour and cornstarch for a few minutes. Add first the chicken broth and then the milk, stirring constantly until the mixture is thickened and smooth. Off heat, beat in the cheese; when it is melted, stir in the seasonings.

3 (10-ounce) packages frozen chopped spinach
3 tablespoons soft butter

2. Cook the spinach according to the directions on the package. Press it dry in a colander and dress it with the butter.

At this point you may stop and continue later. (Refrigerate the sauce in the utensil, covered. Refrigerate the spinach, covered.)

Reserved sauce
2 egg yolks, beaten
1 pound cooked lump crabmeat

3. Over simmering water, bring the sauce to serving temperature in the double boiler. (If you have refrigerated the spinach, reheat it while you are warming the sauce.) Into the heated sauce, beat the egg yolks and then fold in the crabmeat. Return the sauce to serving temperature. On individual heated plates, make a nest of the heated spinach and over it spoon the crabmeat.

Wild Rice

1 cup wild rice

In several waters, rinse the grain, discarding any particles which may rise to the surface.

4 cups water
1 teaspoon salt

In a saucepan, combine the wild rice, water, and salt. Bring the liquid to the boil, reduce the heat, and simmer the wild rice for 45 to 50 minutes, or until it is tender but still somewhat chewy. Drain it well.

Soft butter

With a rubber spatula, fold in softened butter to taste (about 1½ tablespoonsful).

Because wild rice does not lose its texture when cooked, you may refrigerate the dish and reheat, once it has come to room temperature, in the microwave oven (about 3½ minutes at high speed).

Baked Pears

Yield: 4 servings
Preparation: about 15 minutes
Cooking: 5 hours in a 250° F. oven
Chilling time: at least 3 hours
Refrigerates

1 (3-inch) piece cinnamon stick
6 cloves
4 slices lemon
Zest of 1 medium orange
⅔ cup sugar
2 cups dry white wine
1 cup water

1. In a flameproof casserole, combine these ingredients. Bring the mixture to the boil, stirring to dissolve the sugar.

4 firm-fleshed pears (Anjou, Bosc and Comice are good choices), peeled, unstemmed, with a thin slice cut from their bottoms so that they stand upright

2. In the casserole, stand the pears; spoon the syrup over them. Bake the pears at 250° F. for 5 hours, basting them each hour. When the pears are tender but still retain their shape, remove them from the oven; allow them to cool in the syrup, basting them frequently. Transfer them to a serving bowl and strain the syrup over them (or you may reduce the syrup to a thicker consistency before straining it over the pears). Cover and chill them for at least 3 hours.

If you are preparing this recipe for 6 persons, use 6 pears; the ingredients for the syrup will be adequate. If you should prepare the dessert for 8 persons, increase the syrup ingredients by one-half.

Shrimp Newburg for 6

Shrimp Newburg
Rice, page xx
Green Salad with Vinaigrette Sauce (page xxv)
Sherbet of Your Choice

Show off at table as a chafing-dish chef!

A day ahead:

shell, devein, rinse, drain thoroughly, and refrigerate the shrimp, covered

prepare the vinaigrette sauce and refrigerate it

A few hours ahead:

measure out and ready all ingredients for the shrimp recipe; refrigerate the butter, fresh shrimp, egg yolks, and cream

if you are using frozen shrimp, put them in the refrigerator to thaw

measure out and ready all that is needed for the rice

prepare the salad greens and refrigerate them in plastic wrap

Shrimp Newburg

Yield: 6 servings

Preparation: about 40 minutes (including preparing fresh shrimp)

8 tablespoons (1 stick) butter
2 pounds fresh raw shrimp, shelled, deveined, rinsed, and well drained *or* 1½ pounds frozen uncooked shrimp, fully thawed
1 teaspoon paprika
¼ cup Cognac
6 egg yolks, beaten
2 cups heavy cream, heated
Salt, if desired

In a chafing dish, heat the butter and in it cook the shrimp, stirring (until they are opaque and pink) about 6 minutes. Stir in the paprika. In a small utensil, warm the brandy; ignite and pour it over the shrimp. To the egg yolks in a second chafing dish, add the heated cream; cook the mixture, stirring constantly, until it thickens. Pour it over the shrimp, stirring the dish gently to blend it. Adjust the seasoning, if necessary, with a little salt.

Rice

Follow the directions in the recipe for cooking rice. Cook and serve the rice plain, as an accompaniment to the sauce.

Green Salad, Vinaigrette

Use two lettuces. For example, 2 heads of Bibb and 1 head of ruby leaf lettuce present colorfully. Rinse and spin dry the leaves. Tear them into bite-size pieces. Dress the salad with Vinaigrette Sauce, about 1/3 cup.

Sherbet of Your Choice

Lemon sherbet is especially good with this menu, but if you cannot find it (for some reason it is not always readily available), use orange sherbet.

Fresh Vegetable Casserole for 6

Fresh Vegetable Casserole
Muffins, page 35, or French Bread
Strawberry Tart, page 45

For vegetarian lunch or after-theater entertaining.

A day ahead:
ready the vegetables and refrigerate them, covered

make the strawberry tart

A few hours ahead:
prepare steps 1 and 2 of the muffin recipe

Fresh Vegetable Casserole

Yield: 6 servings
Cooking: 20 minutes
Preparation: about 20 minutes

5 tablespoons olive oil
1 large cucumber, peeled, quartered lengthwise, seeded, and cut in 1-inch segments
1 medium eggplant, peeled and cut in cubes (about ¾ inch)
1 small clove garlic, peeled and put through a press
1 large onion, peeled and chopped coarse
1 large ripe tomato, peeled, seeded, and chopped
1 large zucchini, trimmed and cut in ¼-inch rounds
¼ cup dry white wine
2 teaspoons fresh lemon juice
Fresh-ground pepper

In a flameproof serving casserole, heat the olive oil and in it cook the vegetables, stirring, to coat them well with the oil. Over them, pour the wine and lemon juice; add a grinding of pepper. Over medium heat, cook the vegetables, covered, for 10 minutes; remove the cover and continue to cook them for 10 minutes, to evaporate the excess moisture (you may raise the heat a little to speed this step).

Muffins

To prepare the muffins follow the directions in the recipe on page 35. You might vary the flavor for this meal by sifting with the dry ingredients ½ to ¾ teaspoon powdered thyme.

Short Pastry for Strawberry Tart

Work quickly and lightly; handle the dough as little as possible.

Yield: 2 (9-inch) shells; for Strawberry Tart you should halve this recipe

Standing time: 1 hour
Preparation: about 10 minutes
Refrigerates; freezes

2 cups all-purpose flour
1 teaspoon salt

1. In a mixing bowl sift together the flour and salt.

⅓ cup vegetable shortening
⅓ cup butter, cut in small bits

2. To the flour, add the shortening and butter. Using a pastry blender or blending fork or two knives (working with both hands) or your fingertips (working very rapidly), blend the mixture until it forms bits the size of green peas.

⅓ cup ice water

3. By the tablespoonful, sprinkle the ice water over the dough, cutting the mixture with a fork. Stop adding water when you are able to pat the dough lightly into a ball. Wrap the pastry in plastic and refrigerate it for 1 hour. Roll out the dough to your desired thickness, line the pie pan with it, and proceed with the recipe at hand. (Any remaining pastry may be frozen for future use. Wrapped closely in plastic wrap, it will keep for 2 months; allow it to come fully to room temperature before using it.)

Strawberry Tart

Use one-half the preceding recipe for Short Pastry and proceed following the recipe on page 45. Substitute the Short Pastry for the supermarket-purchased shell or graham-cracker crust.

Welsh Rabbit for 4

Welsh Rabbit
Mixed Vegetable Salad, page 7, with Vinaigrette Sauce (page xxv)
Sherbet of Your Choice
Petits Fours

Another lunch to offer with impunity to non-meat-eaters.

A day ahead:

prepare the vinaigrette sauce and refrigerate it

prepare and refrigerate the vegetable salad

grate the cheese for the Welsh rabbit and refrigerate it, covered

Welsh Rabbit

What is the origin of the name? No one really knows. One legend is that the dish substituted for the real rabbit that the inept Welsh husband failed to shoot. Another suggests that "rabbit" is a perversion of "rarebit." I prefer to think that the delicacy is the invention of a creative housewife, slightly put off, perhaps, by her husband's faulty marksmanship.

Yield: 4 servings Doubles
Preparation: about 25 minutes

½ pound Cheddar cheese, grated
¾ cup evaporated milk *or* warm beer (see the note below)
½ to ¾ teaspoon Dijon mustard (to taste)
1 teaspoon Worcestershire sauce
Fresh-ground white pepper
2 egg yolks, if desired (see the note below)

1. In the top of a double boiler, combine all the ingredients except the egg yolks. Over boiling water, cook the mixture, stirring constantly, until the cheese is melted and the rabbit is smooth.

8 buttered toast slices or 4 English muffins, halved

2. Serve the hot cheese on slices of buttered toast or on buttered and toasted English muffins.

4 poached eggs, if desired

3. If desired, you may garnish each serving with the addition of a poached egg—in this case, you have produced what is known as a Golden Buck.

If you prefer, warm beer may be substituted for the evaporated milk, and 2 egg yolks may be beaten into the completed rabbit just as you serve it.

Sherbet of Your Choice

Because of the fairly piquant flavors of the meal, I suggest raspberry sherbet, a bit sweeter than lemon or orange. Accompany the sherbet with petits fours.

Crab Quiche for 6

Crab Quiche
Bibb Lettuce Salad, page 56 with Lemon Vinaigrette Sauce (page xxv)
Apricot Compote
Petits Fours

A day ahead:

prepare the lettuce and refrigerate it in a plastic bag

prepare the lemon vinaigrette sauce and refrigerate it

grate the cheese

toast the almonds

make the apricot compote and refrigerate it, covered

A few hours ahead:

prepare the custard for the quiche; cover and refrigerate it

Crab Quiche

Yield: 6 servings
Preparation: about 30 minutes
Cooking: 15 minutes in a 400° F. oven; 20 minutes at 325° F.

1 cup grated natural Swiss cheese

1. Grate the cheese and reserve it.

3 eggs
1 cup light cream
¼ teaspoon dry mustard
¼ teaspoon mace
2 (7-ounce) cans crabmeat, the tendons discarded
3 scallions, trimmed and chopped fine, with a little of the crisp green part

2. In a mixing bowl, combine the eggs and cream. Using a rotary beater, blend the mixture thoroughly. Add the mustard and mace and beat the mixture once again. Stir in the crabmeat and scallions.

At this point you may stop and continue later. (Cover and refrigerate the mixture and the reserved cheese.)

1 (9-inch) unbaked pastry shell
Reserved Swiss cheese
Prepared egg mixture
1 (3-ounce) package slivered almonds, toasted; you will not need the entire package, but toast them all and store them, closely covered, against future use

3. Over the bottom of the pastry shell, arrange an even layer of the cheese. Over it, spoon the custard mixture. Over the top of the egg mixture, sprinkle as many toasted almonds as you think look appetizing. Bake the quiche at 400° F. for 15 minutes; reduce the heat to 325° F. and continue baking it for 20 minutes, or until the custard is set (a sharp knife inserted at the center will come out clean) and the pastry is golden. Allow the quiche to stand for 5 minutes before serving it.

Bibb Lettuce Salad

Follow the directions in the recipe. Dress the salad with Lemon Vinaigrette Sauce, about ⅓ cup.

Apricot Compote

Yield: 6 servings — Doubles; refrigerates
Preparation: about 20 minutes

1 (11-ounce) package tenderized dried apricots
½ cup dry white wine
Water
2 slices lemon
Sugar

In a saucepan, combine the apricots and wine. Add water to cover and the lemon slices. Bring the liquid to the boil; reduce the heat, and simmer the apricots, uncovered, for about 12 minutes, or until they are tender; they should not be mushy. Discard the lemon slices and stir in sugar to taste.

Beef-Filled Mushrooms for 6

Beef-Filled Mushrooms
Orzo
Mixed Lettuce and Spinach Salad with the Vinaigrette Sauce (page xxv) of Your Choice
Chocolate Pots de Crème

A day ahead:

prepare the salad ingredients and refrigerate them in separate plastic bags

prepare the vinaigrette sauce

make the *pots de crème*

A few hours ahead:

complete steps 1, 2, and 3 of the mushroom recipe; cover and refrigerate the mushrooms

Beef-Filled Mushrooms

Yield: 6 servings as a main course; 8 servings, should you sometime wish to serve them as an appetizer

Preparation: about 30 minutes
Cooking: about 5 minutes in a preheated broiler

24 large, perfect mushrooms, stemmed (reserve the stems for future use)
Melted butter

1. Dip the mushrooms in melted butter and set them aside.

1½ pounds ground round (ask your butcher to grind it twice)
½ cup tomato sauce
1 small clove garlic, peeled and put through a press
Grated rind of 1 small lemon
½ teaspoon tarragon
¼ teaspoon thyme
¾ teaspoon salt, if desired
Fresh-ground pepper

2. In a mixing bowl, combine and blend thoroughly these eight ingredients.

Reserved mushroom caps

3. With the mixture, fill the mushroom caps so that they are well rounded (you will find it easier to make meat balls and then flatten one side to fit in the mushroom). Arrange the mushrooms on a broiling rack.

At this point you may stop and continue later. (Cover and refrigerate the mushrooms on the broiling rack. Remove them from the refrigerator in time for them to reach room temperature before cooking.)

4. In a preheated broiler, cook the mushrooms for about 5 minutes, or until the beef has reached your desired degree of doneness.

Orzo (Rice-Shaped Pasta)

For 4 servings, allow 1 cup uncooked orzo. In a large saucepan, bring to the boil several quarts lightly salted water. Add 2 or 3 tablespoons oil (to help prevent the pasta from sticking), then add the orzo and cook it over high heat, uncovered, for 8 to 10 minutes, or until it is just tender; do not overcook it. Drain it in a sieve and into it stir 2 or 3 tablespoons soft butter and fine-chopped parsley to taste.

If you are serving 6 persons. use 1½ cups orzo; 2 cups will serve 8.

Mixed Lettuce and Spinach Salad

For 6 servings, use 1 large head leaf lettuce, a few cherry tomatoes, halved, a small red onion, peeled, sliced, and divided into rings, and several tender spinach leaves for color contrast. Rinse and thoroughly spin dry the lettuce and the spinach. Tear the leaves into bite-size pieces. Dress the salad with a vinaigrette sauce of your choice, page xxv.

Chocolate Pots de Crème

Yield: 6 servings
Preparation: about 15 minutes

Chilling time: 4 hours
Doubles; refrigerates

1 (6-ounce) package semi-sweet chocolate bits
2 eggs
¼ cup chocolate- *or* coffee-flavored liqueur

1. In the container of a blender, combine these three ingredients and whirl them briefly, about 5 seconds.

2 tablespoons sugar
½ cup milk

2. In a saucepan, combine the sugar and milk. Bring the mixture to a rolling boil, taking care that it does not boil over. With the motor of the blender running, pour the boiling milk in a steady stream over the chocolate bits. Blend the mixture until it is smooth. Pour the dessert into small dishes or dessert cups and chill it for at least 4 hours, or until it is thoroughly set.

FOR VARIATION:
Chocolate* Pots de Crème *with Rum: Instead of chocolate- or coffee-flavored liqueur use ¼ cup dark rum.

Chicken and Artichoke Hearts in Cream for 4

Chicken and Artichoke Hearts in Cream
Wild Rice, page xxi
Green Salad with Lemon Vinaigrette Sauce (page xxv)
Pineapple in Orange Syrup, page 56
Petits Fours

A day ahead:

complete step 1 of the chicken recipe

prepare the scallions and mushrooms for step 3 of the chicken recipe; refrigerate them in separate plastic bags

make the pineapple in orange syrup

prepare the salad greens and refrigerate them in a plastic bag

prepare the lemon vinaigrette sauce and refrigerate it

A few hours ahead:

cook the wild rice

remove the artichoke hearts from the refrigerator

Chicken and Artichoke Hearts in Cream

Yield: 4 servings
Preparation: about 30 minutes
Cooking: about 12 minutes
Doubles; refrigerates

1 (9-ounce) package frozen artichoke hearts
2 large full skinless, boneless chicken breasts, trimmed of all fat

1. Cook the artichoke hearts according to the directions on the package; drain and reserve them. Halve the chicken breasts lengthwise.

At this point you may stop and continue later. (Refrigerate the artichokes and the chicken, closely covered.)

3 tablespoons butter

2. In a skillet, heat the butter and in it, over moderately high heat, sauté the chicken breasts (turning them once) for about 6 minutes, or until they are resilient when pressed. Remove and reserve them.

2 scallions, trimmed and chopped fine, with a little of the crisp green part
12 button mushrooms, trimmed and sliced
¼ cup Cognac
½ cups heavy cream
Salt, if desired
Fresh-ground white pepper
Reserved artichoke hearts
Reserved chicken

3. To the butter remaining in the skillet, add the scallions and mushrooms; cook them briefly, stirring. In a small utensil, warm the Cognac; ignite it and pour it over the mushrooms. When the flame dies, stir in the cream and, over high heat, allow the sauce to cook down for 5 minutes. Adjust the seasoning to taste. Add the artichoke hearts and chicken breasts, spooning the sauce over them. Over gentle heat, bring the dish to serving temperature.

Green Salad, Lemon Vinaigrette

Use a combination of 2 or 3 tender-leaf lettuces (about 24 leaves total). Rinse and thoroughly spin dry the leaves; tear them into bite-size pieces. Because the main dish is rich, you do not need a complicated side dish. Dress the salad with Lemon Vinaigrette Sauce, about ⅓ cup.

Crêpes de Volaille, Mornay, for 6

Crêpes de Volaille with Mornay Sauce (page xviii)
Green Peas, page 47
Cherries Jubilee

2 days ahead:

make the crêpes (unless you already have them on hand, frozen)

poach the chicken breast and refrigerate it, tightly wrapped in plastic

A day ahead:

complete steps 1, 2, 3, and 4 of the crêpes de volaille recipe

complete steps 1 and 2 of the cherries jubilee recipe

A few hours ahead:

remove all the prepared items from the refrigerator so they will be at room temperature

prepare the peas

Crêpes de Volaille, Mornay

Yield: 6 servings
Preparation: about 1½ hours (total, and at different times)
Cooking: 12 minutes in a 400° F. oven
Doubles; refrigerates; freezes

1 recipe (18) Crêpes
1 recipe Mornay Sauce

Crêpes

If you wish to make more than 18 crêpes (and you may, for they can be kept frozen as long as six months—thus providing a quick and pleasant meal made from leftovers), make the recipe twice; do not try to double it.

Yield: about 18 crêpes
Preparation and cooking: about 1 hour
Standing time: at least 2 hours
Refrigerates; freezes

½ cup flour
½ teaspoon salt
2 eggs
¾ cup milk
¾ cup water
5 tablespoons butter, melted and slightly cooled

1. In the container of a blender, combine these ingredients and, on medium speed, whirl them for 20 seconds, or until the mixture is completely homogeneous. With a rubber spatula, scrape down the sides of the container so that all of the ingredients are incorporated in the finished batter. Allow it to stand for at least 2 hours (in the refrigerator, if desired) before cooking the crêpes.

Soft butter

2. Heat and butter lightly a 5- or 6-inch skillet or crêpe pan. Pour in batter barely to cover the bottom of the pan (about 3 tablespoons); tilt the pan to spread the batter evenly. Cook the crêpes as if they were pancakes, first one side and then the other, turning them with a spatula.

3. To refrigerate for 1 week's storage or to freeze crêpes, allow them to cool and then stack them with a piece of waxed paper between each (to prevent their sticking together); wrap the stack in plastic wrap.

Filling for the Crêpes

4 tablespoons butter
2 shallots, peeled and chopped fine
¼ cup fine-chopped parsley
¾ pound mushrooms, trimmed and chopped

1. In a skillet, heat the butter and in it briefly cook the shallots and parsley. Add the mushrooms and, over gentle heat, cook them, stirring occasionally, until the excess moisture is evaporated.

1 cup diced cooked chicken breast (about 1 medium full breast)
Grated rind of 1 lemon
½ cup Mornay sauce (reserve the remaining sauce)
Salt, if desired
Fresh-ground white pepper

2. Into the contents of the skillet, stir the chicken. Add the lemon rind, sauce, and season the mixture to taste.

Reserved crêpes

3. Onto each crêpe, spoon about 2 tablespoons of the chicken mixture. Roll the crêpes and arrange them, seam side down, in a lightly buttered oven-proof serving dish.

At this point you may stop and continue later. (Cover the dish closely with plastic wrap and refrigerate it. Refrigerate the remaining Mornay sauce, well covered. Remove the prepared crêpes and Mornay sauce from the refrigerator so that they will be at room temperature when you cook them.)

Reserved Mornay sauce
1 egg yolk

4. Into the remaining Mornay sauce, beat the egg yolk. Over the crêpes, spoon the sauce. Bake the dish at 400° F. for about 12 minutes, or until the sauce is bubbly.

FOR VARIATION:
Dessert Crêpes: Make the crêpes as directed above, adding to the list of ingredients ¼ cup confectioners' sugar and 1 teaspoon vanilla or 3 tablespoons Cognac or 3 tablespoons orange-flavored liqueur.

1. Reserve the prepared crêpes, and Mornay sauce.

Cherries Jubilee

Yield: 6 servings
Preparation: about 15 minutes
Cooking: 10 minutes
Doubles; refrigerates

1 tablespoon cornstarch
3 tablespoons sugar
A few grains of salt, if desired
2 (1-pound) cans pitted dark sweet cherries, drained; reserve the liquid
Ruby port wine

1. In a saucepan, blend the cornstarch, sugar, and salt, if desired. Blend the reserved cherry liquid with port to equal 2 cups. Add the mixture to the contents of the saucepan, stirring to blend it well.

Zest of 1 lemon, cut in julienne strips
Zest of 1 orange, cut in julienne strips
Water to cover
Reserved cherries
2 tablespoons strained fresh lemon juice

2. In a second saucepan, combine the lemon and orange zests, add water to cover, bring it to the boil, and cook the zest, uncovered, for 5 minutes.

Drain it and add it to the contents of the saucepan. Cook the sauce, stirring, until it is thickened and smooth. Stir in the cherries and lemon juice.

At this point you may stop and continue later. (Refrigerate the sauce, covered.)

½ cup Cognac
Vanilla ice cream (about 2 quarts)

3. Bring the sauce to serving temperature and transfer it to a flameproof serving dish. To present the dessert, warm the Cognac in a small utensil, ignite it, and pour it over the cherry sauce. While the sauce is still flaming, spoon it over individual servings of the ice cream.

Cheese Fondue for 4

Cheese Fondue
French Bread
Bibb Lettuce Salad, page 56, with Lemon Vinaigrette Sauce (page xxv)
Dried-Fruit Compote (page 19)

Fondue, a national dish of Switzerland, makes for a festive meal especially suitable for winter. There is nothing formal about everyone's dunking his or her bread into the communal pot of melted cheese. It is customarily cooked in a caquelon, a highly fired and glazed pottery saucepan (an enamelized-iron saucepan works equally well) and kept heated over a spirit lamp or similar appliance. Fondue forks—long-handled, two- or three-tined forks making easy the spearing and dipping of the bread—are readily available, even at many specialty food stores. The fondue should be embellished by only the simplest accompaniments.

A day ahead:

prepare the lettuce and refrigerate it in a plastic bag

make the lemon vinaigrette sauce and refrigerate it

make the dried-fruit compote

grate the cheeses and refrigerate them closely covered with plastic wrap

A few hours ahead:

peel the garlic and wrap it in plastic wrap

measure out the remaining ingredients for the fondue

cut the bread in bite-size pieces and reserve it in a plastic bag

remove the cheeses from the refrigerator

Cheese Fondue

Among my closest friends are the Debeljevics, who live in Gottlieben, Switzerland, a village that looks like the stage set of a child's play. Before her retirement from the international operatic scene, Mrs. Debeljevic was better known as Lisa Della Casa, one of the great prima donnas of the nineteen-fifties and -sixties. Together with her attractive husband, Dragan, and their warm-hearted daughter, Vesna, Lisa now makes her home in a thirteenth-century schloss once owned as a hunting lodge by Emperor Napoleon III.

I have spent many happy hours of good talk and homely contentment there, but I have no warmer memory than that of our sitting around the kitchen table eating the meal for which I give the menu below. While the ingredients for the fondue are listed in the usual format, the instructions are repeated as Vesna wrote them for me.

Yield: 4 servings
Preparation: about 25 minutes
Cooking: about 20 minutes

1 large clove garlic, peeled and split lengthwise
A large glazed-earthenware or enamelized-iron saucepan

1. "First you rub the fondue pot with a clove of garlic—long, thoroughly, and pressing hard, and making sure you cover every bit of the pot well."

½ pound Gruyère cheese, grated
½ pound Emmenthaler cheese, grated
¼ pound Appenzeller cheese, grated
1½ cups dry white wine
3 or 4 cloves garlic

2. In the saucepan, combine the cheeses and wine and, over moderate heat, "using a wooden spoon, stir constantly yet carefully (as it splashes out easily and smells awful when hitting the stove). I forgot to say, before you start to stir, Mother always adds 3 or 4 cloves of pressed garlic, depending upon your taste."

3 tablespoons cornstarch, mixed until smooth with
¼ cup *Kirschwasser*
Fresh-ground white pepper
Fresh-grated nutmeg

3. "Once the cheese has become fluid, let as much of this mixture [cornstarch-and-*Kirsch*—author] flow into the fondue as is necessary to bind the cheese and wine in a creamy consistency. Now you can spice with as much pepper from the mill and nutmeg as you like."

Thick-crusted French bread, cut in substantial bite-size pieces
1 cup *Kirschwasser*, if desired (divided equally among four small sauce dishes)

4. "As a bread, use a white one with much crust to be able to pierce with your fork through the white into the crust, to prevent losing it while eating. Each lost piece requires the loser to pay for a bottle of wine. What a cheerful round! We in the family have the habit of briefly dipping each piece of bread into *Kirsch* before dipping it into the cheese."

Index